Cry Out Of Russia

escape from darkness

by

Anna Fischer

Trafford
PUBLISHING®

Order this book online at www.trafford.com
or email orders@trafford.com

Most Trafford titles are also available at major online book retailers.

Note for Librarians: A cataloguing record for this book is available from Library
and Archives Canada at www.collectionscanada.ca/amicus/index-e.html

Printed in Victoria, BC, Canada.

ISBN: 978-1-4269-1317-4 (sc)

*We at Trafford believe that it is the responsibility of us all, as both individuals
and corporations, to make choices that are environmentally and socially sound.
You, in turn, are supporting this responsible conduct each time you purchase a
Trafford book, or make use of our publishing services. To find out how you are
helping, please visit www.trafford.com/responsiblepublishing.html*

*Our mission is to efficiently provide the world's finest, most comprehensive
book publishing service, enabling every author to experience success.
To find out how to publish your book, your way, and have it available
worldwide, visit us online at www.trafford.com*

Trafford rev. 6/3/2009

Trafford
PUBLISHING® www.trafford.com

North America & international
toll-free: 1 888 232 4444 (USA & Canada)
phone: 250 383 6864 ♦ fax: 250 383 6804 ♦ email: info@trafford.com

The United Kingdom & Europe
phone: +44 (0)1865 487 395 ♦ local rate: 0845 230 9601
facsimile: +44 (0)1865 481 507 ♦ email: info.uk@trafford.com

10 9 8 7 6 5 4 3 2 1

Author's Biography

I was born on August 12, 1926 in Johannestal, Ukraine. This was my home until 1944. During World War ll we fled to the West and arrived in Poland, from there we were transported by train to West Germany. In 1951, I immigrated to Canada, first arriving in Halifax, Nova Scotia, then traveling by train to Leader, Saskatchewan, where relatives were awaiting my arrival.

From there my journey led me to Medicine Hat, Alberta. On August 12,1955, I married Frederick Fischer, settling in Horsham, Saskatchewan, where we farmed. After the death of my husband on November 22, 1969, I moved to Medicine Hat, Alberta with my four children, where I still reside.

This is the first book I have written. It is mainly for my family and friends to share, and to keep the memories alive.

A NOTE FROM THE AUTHOR

This book was written from the recollection of my own experiences and family member's stories as they were described to me. The wording and phrasing of the sentences may not be sophisticated or professional, but is written from the heart.

The events in this book are factual accounts of what happened to my family and myself. The experiences that I have endured during the dates indicated are true to the best of my memories and knowledge as the events unfolded.

This biography depicts the horrifying experiences of thousands of human beings, including my grandparents and relatives. I too, personally experienced the brutal dictatorship, under the rule of Stalin's Communist Regime in Russia. Under this regime the people suffered poverty, torture, despair, murder and starvation.

Everyone that has experienced living under the Communist Regime in Russia have his or her own stories to tell.

In Loving
Memory of
My Parents
Karl & Otaria Roth

ACKNOWLEDGEMENTS

I would like to thank my daughters, Audrey and Melinda, for the arduous hours spent editing and typing. Special appreciation to Myrna Wooley and Helen Shurvell for proofreading the final draft before printing.

A special recognition to so many people that gave me the encouragement I needed to continue writing this book.

Cover Design by Dale W. Fischer

CONTENTS

Introduction

Thousands of humans experienced misery for many long years during the war without seeing an end to the tunnel of darkness. Many who were fortunate to survive the brutality, preferred not to talk about their experiences. The memories were too painful and it was easier just to block the past from their lives.

The heartbreaking memories will be a constant reminder for the rest of their lives, never to be forgotten. Some have chosen to take these experiences of misery, torture and starvation to their graves.

I too have experienced the torture and sorrow that came with living under Stalin's regime – from the state-imposed famine of 1932 – 1933 to becoming, in 1944, a displaced person of WW11. They were grueling years.

Like all the rest, I too tried to forget the misery of the past, trying to convince myself by thinking and saying, "Thank God I am alive". In my heart I felt the pain for so many of our loved ones who had to endure and face such gruesome deaths. Small innocent children had to die cruel, needless deaths. The unanswered question is, "Why?"

Although plagued with sadness, I tried to forget my experiences, wiping my mind of these memories as much as possible. After many years of painful struggle, I had successfully managed to avoid my feelings of heartache. For years I fooled myself. The fear instilled in the German population led us to live silent, terrible lives under the Stalin Regime. You learned quickly that the more tight-lipped you were, the better chance of survival you had. These painful experiences stayed with us and will continue to be a part of our lives forever.

Buried in my mind for many years was the memory of brutality and utter horror. I was compelled to bring forth these memories of the loved ones who had to die in Northern Siberia (the coldest part of Russia). With a troubled conscience, I could no longer bear the silence.

By revealing my experiences I was able to emerge from the darkest time of my life into a life of light. My invitation to the GRHS Convention in Rapid City, SD on Sept 4 - 7/2003 encouraged me to continue my writing.

When asked to be a participant in the panel discussion I felt very fortunate and it gave me the confidence and strength to share my life experiences before a live audience. I felt honored to be able to partake in the Germans From Russia Convention. As well, I had the opportunity to meet many of my relatives.

Finally, I was able to break the chain, to really feel the freedom in my life.

I truly appreciate living in a free country with freedom of speech. For the first time in my life I can now talk about our lives in the dark past. It gives me a great feeling to be able to express myself and to reveal my story.

1
New Beginnings

My Great, Great Grandparents emigrated from
Germany to the Promised Land, Russia. During the
Imperial Time, my great-great grandfather, John Roth, his
wife Dorothy and son (Ludwig) emigrated from Prussia,
Germany by wagon and on foot. In approximately 1819
they arrived and settled in Russia. Since Ludwig was only
two years old, he rode on the homemade wooden wagon,
which was pulled by the sheer strength of his parents.

Ludwig was my Great Grandfather, and his wife
Wilhelmina Roth (nee Heinle) was my Great Grandmother.
They had eleven children (Gottlieb, Christian, Johan,
Carolina, Fredericka, Wilhelmina, Fredrich, Karl, Michael,
Ludwig and Wilhelm).

Wilhelm Roth, was my grandfather...my
grandmother was Katharina Roth (nee Zimmerman). They
had five children (Gottlieb, Rosa, Wilhelm, Karl and
Heinrich).

Karl Roth was my father; my mother was Otaria
Roth (nee Belanov). They had seven children Anna,
Gottlieb, Adolf, Hilda, Katharina, Rosa and Helene (oldest
to youngest).

I am Anna, the oldest daughter of Karl and Otaria
Roth born on August 12, 1926 in Johannestal, Ukraine. My
grandparents had settled in Johannestal. This is where the
story of my life starts. My memoirs contain the stories and
experiences of our fathers' and forefathers' lives. Our

forefathers left their beloved birthplace, the homeland of Germany, to find a new home in Russia…the so-called Motherland. As it was told, the resettlement started when Catharina the Great ruled Russia. At that time there were calls and offers made from the Empress's throne for immigrants from Germany to enter Russia. Immigration was also open to many other countries. People were encouraged to take the chance to immigrate to Russia. Russia required skilled hard-working people and the Germans were approached first. The promises made sounded good, very encouraging and rewarding. The Germans were full of optimism and expectations and did not fear the work that lay ahead of them. Since Germany is such a small country and the Counts and Royalty owned most of the land, there was no possibility for the people to ever own their own land. Besides, the hardships of sustaining their families left many people with no future. Many of our forefathers answered the calls from Russia and moved for the well being of their families and futures.

Our forefathers immigrated to Russia in the 1700's and 1850's and beyond these years. The families banded together and left in groups. It was a difficult time for families, many with small children traveling on foot. The passage to Russia was long and wearisome. As promised, the settlers were to obtain free land from the government. The cattle owner, Yeschitzkie, used the land that was allotted to the German immigrants, originally belonging to the Imperial Crown, to graze cattle. The term of repayment to the government was over a 10-year period, interest free. Freedom to practice their own religious beliefs and military free services for 100 years were also part of the promises made to entice immigration. The terms sounded promising and encouraging; our forefathers kept faith and relied completely in their hopes of a better life. Once they reached Russian soil, the so-called new home, families were assigned to various locations, mostly in the Kerson area close to the Black Sea. Hence the name, Black Sea Germans evolved. Although the flat terrain, treeless plains and barren underdeveloped landscape were a cause for despair, the German Immigrants were happy to start a new life for themselves. The area looked much like our Canadian prairies. In Russian this region was referred to as, "Die Steppe".

Families settled on their assigned homesteads. Development was difficult as the proper tools and equipment required to till the land were not available and frustration escalated. If money had been accessible, some of our forefathers would have considered going back to their homeland of Germany. So they labored on and tried making their living off the land. Filled with pride and hope they looked forward to building their future.

For families who had brought some wealth with them life was easier and progress much faster. Most of the German people borrowed money from the Czar regime to purchase the equipment needed for farming.

The Empire had confidence in the German settlers; they were very hard working people and put their heart and soul into their work. The Russian government soon became aware that the German settlers were skilled farmers with plenty of knowledge in agriculture.

Now was the time to convert their new homesteads into a productive piece of land. The soil in this region was very rich and fertile, for it had never been broken or tilled.

After the land had been divided, the families stuck together and helped each other with seeding and harvesting. The construction of basic housing started slowly. The small houses were made of loam, short straw and water. This mixture was brought to a thick porridge like consistency, which was made by stomping with bare feet. As a child, I remember the same technique being used. We thought this was fun and didn't even realize this was a great help in the production of the small houses. Because of the weather, frequent repairs were necessary. In heavy rainfalls the water would wash away the mud and in extreme heat the mud would crack leaving openings on the rooftops and walls. We were given the task of filling in the holes on the sides and roof of the house with mud, thinking how much fun it was to play with mud. These small mud houses consisted of two small rooms. One room was a kitchen and the other room was used as a sitting room, which was converted to a bedroom that was occupied by the whole family. The houses in the Russian language were called "Samelankas". Many times parents lived with their children and their families. Everyone looked after one another. They were happy to have a warm place to stay over the winter, which were dreadfully cold where we lived. Our ancestors had to become accustomed to their surroundings. They were not prepared for the colder weather. The clothes they wore were not suitable for the weather conditions. Many women were without heavy winter coats, having only a long "Halztuch", which was somewhat like a large shawl for keeping warm. Spring arrived early in the Black Sea area of the Ukraine. Each family would plant a garden, which provided fresh vegetables, potatoes, carrots, beets and cabbage. During the winter months, the vegetables were stored in underground cellars, which were dug by hand. These cellars were dug about nine feet deep in the ground, with steps leading to the bottom. The cellars were covered with thick brush and topped with a layer of straw and dirt to keep them cold for storage. The Russian dish, borscht, which is a soup made with vegetables, was adopted quickly by the German people.

A church and school were soon erected allowing the settlers to practice their faith and children could attend school. The streets were designed to form a small village. Their hard labor had paid off; their dreams finally came true.

In the spring, around March, most of the settlers were out in the fields planting the crops, using oxen or horses. The smaller pieces of land were seeded by hand. The sickle and scythe were used to harvest the crops in fall. The swaths were brought to the threshing location, which was called "Harman" in Russian. The grain with the straw was laid out in a circle a few feet thick. The horses then walked in a circle pulling a heavy stone slab over the grain till the wheat had separated from the straw. The wheat was cleaned with a hand operated cleaning mill. It was slow, tedious work. Gathering together and discussing the days' work while eating sunflower seeds was the local men's socializing for the end of the day. The main crops grown were wheat, barley, oats, corn and sunflowers. The nearest sunflower rendering mill was in the village of Adamovka, approximately forty kilometers from Johannestal. There, the oil was extracted from the sunflower seeds. Because of the distance, farmers had to make accommodations to stay overnight for themselves and their horses. In the village of Johannestal there were no mills of any kind. The wheat had to be taken to the flourmill in the village of Landau, ten kilometers from Johannestal, where the wheat was made into flour.

On average, the families were large and as the children grew up they took care of the elderly. With no radio or newspaper, they depended on socializing with family and friends for entertainment.

Any type of medical knowledge was unavailable. There were no doctors in the area and very little medication to be found. The sick relied on home remedies to cure their ailments. Sometimes illness would wipe entire families.

The German settlers named most villages in the Ukraine after the places they had left behind in Germany, or they would even name the village after the first settler. It is believed that Johannestal was named after the first settler. His name was Johan. Tal came from the German language, which means "a valley or a coulee". As the population grew, Johannestal was also divided into the upper and lower village. A stone quarry was situated in the lower part of the village. This quarry provided the soft sandstone, which was used for building. Right in the middle of the village was a school, a Lutheran church and the General Store. The villagers of Johannestal had a Lutheran background. Later some people strayed from their Lutheran faith and a Baptist Congregation was formed. Selected individuals who had great knowledge of the Bible and the word of God officiated the church services. Most of our forefathers were quite religious and had much faith in God's word. They studied and read the scriptures faithfully. Sunday was the day for church and rest; nobody worked! Uncle Gottlieb, my father's older brother, worked in the General Store, but not on Sundays.

The German people always helped each other with the farming and with other day-to-day duties. Villagers became self-sufficient with their own blacksmith, carpenter, and shoemaker. It was still cheaper to patch the torn and ripped shoes than buy new ones.

As the village grew, my Uncle Gottlieb had to frequently travel to the city of Odessa to stock the store with supplies. Odessa was on the shore of the Black Sea. Most goods were shipped to Odessa crossing the Black Sea. He would leave by horse and wagon and travel approximately 100 kilometers to reach his destination. . These trips were long and exhausting, as there were no decent roads, especially when it was raining. It was virtually impossible to cross the deep Yeschitzkie Valley. Quite often the rain and mud forced him to stay overnight in the village of Neusatz Futter. A resting place for the horse and wagon could also be found there. A man named Bitterman owned the lodging he stayed at. This is where my Uncle Gottlieb met his future wife, Katharina Bitterman. During one of these trips he had overheard a conversation about plans for leaving Russia and immigrating to America. Because of Uncle Gottliebs' occupation, he was fortunate to have connections with the right people. The threat of war was on the rise and fear of the draft was intensifying. The German people were frightened of the uncertainty in their lives and immigrating to the USA looked and sounded promising and safe.

My uncle Gottlieb listened to all this talk of the USA and considered the prospect very seriously. After my uncle had returned from Odessa, he discussed moving to the

USA, expressing his reservations about the war. He told his parents everything he had heard about the threat of war and he was sure to be drafted. At nineteen, he was the right age for being enlisted in the Russian Army. His parents listened with great concern. My grandparents were troubled that their son would leave. But my Uncle Gottlieb said to his parents, "Don't worry, I won't be alone". Many people had made applications to immigrate to the USA where many of our relatives resided. Uncle Gottlieb was determined to go. He completed the required papers and eventually was accepted to immigrate to the United States in the year 1909. Gottlieb Roth left his parents and siblings for America.

2
The Fall of Russia
(1911-1918)

The journey to America was an enormous undertaking for my Uncle Gottlieb, crossing the great ocean to a destination so foreign to him. The trip was a long one as the ship was not large and sailed slowly. When he finally arrived on American soil he was relieved that the journey was behind him. His parents and family received the good news that their son had arrived safe and sound in America. At this point he was with relatives in North Dakota, USA. His parents could now relax, knowing everything was fine. After a short time in North Dakota, my uncle found work with intentions of helping his family out financially. Most of the relatives had immigrated to the Dakotas in previous years; this made it most desirable for Uncle Gottlieb to stay in this area. To his dismay, the quota for immigrants had already been filled, and free land was no longer available to new immigrants in the North Dakota area.

The word had spread quickly about Canada. Land was still available and not as heavily populated. In 1911, Uncle Gottlieb, his Uncle John Roth and John Eichale, along with several other men, set off for the journey north to Canada. Arriving by train in the small town of Maple Creek, Saskatchewan where the immigration office was located at the time. The immigrants were directed to their particular destinations. My Uncle Gottlieb was assigned to go north of Maple Creek, where he made his new home in the area of Burstall, Saskatchewan. It certainly was not going to be easy; having to build a life and home on the untamed soil just as his forefathers had to do when emigrating from Germany to Russia.

Every beginning is hard and difficult. Katharina Bitterman and her family had immigrated to America around the same time as my Uncle Gottlieb; so in 1915, my uncle and Katharina were married. My Uncle's hopes were kept high that his parents and family would also be permitted to immigrate to Canada. The remaining family that stayed behind consisted of his parents Wilhelm and Katharina Roth, three brothers Wilhelm, Karl, and Heinrich, and one sister Rosa. They all had hoped that one day they too would have the chance to follow their brother Gottlieb and make their home in Canada.

Unfortunately, God had planned another destiny for them. During this time the situation in Russia had become even more unsettled. In 1914 Russia, with Czar Nicholas II leading the country entered the First World War with very ill prepared armed forces and an economy that could not handle the demands of war. The defeat in 1915-1916 discredited his regime and forced his abdication in March of 1917. This was followed by the Bolshevik seizure of power in November 1917. July 1918 minor functionaries of the new regime brutally murdered Czar Nicholas II and the entire Royal family.

After the Bolshevik seizure of power, times of distress were becoming more prominent. The German people were being mistreated. Although the German people had made Russia their home for generations, they were accused of espionage and treason toward the country. Life had to go on; for many Germans, Russia was home, their birthplace. Once the Communist Party took over from the Bolshevik Regime, things took a turn for the worse with the rise of the most feared and ruthless leader that reigned over all of Russia – Joseph Stalin.

My father told me that his parents were very poor. His family lived with poverty and hunger. My poor ragged father went begging from door to door. He'd beg for a piece of bread or perhaps some potatoes to take home to his hungry family. My grandfather Wilhelm Roth was dying a slow death of starvation. I can imagine how desperate and hungry my grandfather must have been to ask his wife if he could butcher the only cow they had so they wouldn't starve. She didn't think it a good idea; at least with the cow alive, they would have a little bit of milk. My grandfather was optimistic that a better time would come, but unfortunately it never came in his lifetime. The American Relief Administration fed millions of Russians every day and provided medical aid however, this help never reached the rural areas. My grandfather Roth died of starvation in 1922 in the motherland of Russia. My grandfather's dying last words were of how hungry he was. He said, "Ich habe so hunger". My grandmother continued to live in poverty and starvation until her death in 1927 in Russia as well.

In Canada my Uncle Gottlieb heard the cries of despair. He began making efforts to apply to immigration with intentions of bringing all of his family members out of Russia to Canada. In 1928, my Uncle Wilhelm, Aunt Christina, and cousins Martha, Gottlieb, Louise and Emanuel, were granted permission to immigrate to Canada. The families that were left behind hoped and prayed that their wish would also be fulfilled.

The changes in the country came so quickly; soon

nobody was allowed to leave the country. The regime
didn't want the outside world to know of the Russian state
of affairs. Communication to the outside world had ceased.
No mail was permitted in or out of Russia. The people
were in shock and lived in fear of the unknown. All
applications to immigrate overseas were refused and no one
was allowed to leave the country. All photographs were
prohibited. People hid any pictures they possessed in their
homes. Religion was forbidden, and bibles were hidden. I
remember my father having a photo of his brother Gottlieb
and the family bible in his possession, which he hid in the
attic of our house. The photo was of Uncle Gottlieb Roth
when he left for Canada. The hidden photos were water
damaged due to the years of rain that had leaked through
the roof.

Stalin was the dictator that brought misery to the
human race throughout Russia. Stalin was very successful at
stripping and crippling the German population of their well
being. One thing he was not able to take away with all his
power and might was the silent prayers of the people. This
was the one possession the people carried with them in
their hearts, and thousands to their graves, no one could
take it from them.

The German people were burdened with heavy
taxes. The wealthier the people were, the more they were
taxed. It depended on how much land or capital a family
owned or how large your house was. It was very difficult
for people to pay these high taxes. I remember as a young
child, overhearing the worrisome conversation my parents
were having. They were concerned how they would be able
to pay the taxes on our dwelling. We no longer owned land,
and the only thing we were allowed to have was our one

cow. Now the regime established the "Collective" which meant all produce belonged to the state. In 1930, the villagers had to hand the land over to the collective farms, and the biggest worries now were how to feed that one cow over the winter months with so very little feed. After the harvest and threshing time was done in the fall, some of the straw was handed out to the families, which was to last for feeding the cow and heating the house over the winter months. We would also gather cow patties by the dams where the cows drank. The patties would be burned to heat the house. In winter my parents would venture out in the deep snow and bring home dried branches in bundles on their backs and use it to heat the home. There was never enough supply of wood to burn to keep the houses warm.

My father and his youngest brother Heinrich Roth wrote to his brother Gottlieb in Canada in 1929:

"Dear Brother Gottlieb and sister-in-law Katharina, please I beg you for help. We are in a terrible time with nothing to eat and no warm clothing to wear. I sit here and write to you brother, my fingers are crippled up from freezing and the window stuffed up with paper, the walls are thick with frost. I don't know how we can survive this cold weather. Dear brother, we are hungry and cold …please help, help us! I am forced to quit writing, the little gas in our lamp is running out. I must say good night brother.
Wilhelm & Katarina".

I believe my Uncle Gottlieb received this last letter from his Sister Rosa in 1929. An angel must have guided this letter to her brother in Canada. This is what the letter had said:

"Dear Brother Gottlieb and Sister-In-Law Katharina and family,
I pray that my letter will arrive in safe hands. This may be the last letter I will be permitted to write you. It is dangerous and I want to let you know that we are enduring a terrible and hopeless time. Only our dear God knows what lies ahead for us and how long we can endure. Our future is in God's hands.
Brother Gottlieb, just as I am writing this letter to you, Brother Karl and Heinrich have walked through the door. My God if you could only see them. Both brothers are standing in rags. Karl is wearing a pair of old shoes with hardly any soles left. Brother Heinrich stands barefoot…no shoes to wear. One can see the hunger in both their eyes. There is nothing for them to eat in the house. It hurts not to be able to give them something and there are no promises of things getting better.
My Dear Brother Gottlieb, you can be thankful that you don't have to endure this misery and suffering. Although your life has not been easy for you either, at least you don't need to go to bed hungry and live in fear of the uncertainty. We live with the fear of which hour of the night you will be led away from your family into the unknown…never returning. Not being able to say good-bye to your children. For us unfortunate people this is our destiny. Our lives are in God's hands from your sister,

" Rosa with family"

My father Karl, his youngest brother Heinrich and

16

sister Rosa were now left behind. They were very close; thank God they still had each other. They were able to empty their hearts to each other, discussing their needs and sorrows.

3
Hardships In Johannestal
(1920-1932)

My childhood memories hold fear and anguish. We as children didn't have the opportunity to know any other reality than poverty and hunger. Looking back at my past, I realize how sad and lonely my childhood was along with the thousands of other children living during this difficult time. My school days were filled without hope. Day after day we went to school, always hungry. Our minds were preoccupied with food or the lack of it and not on our studies. Praise from the teachers was a rarity. After school, we came home to an empty house, as mothers were at work in the Collective from morning until dark. After the women arrived home, there was more work waiting for them. There was very little time for our parents to spend with their children, and no time to rest. I know our parents loved us deeply, but they were drained from the days work and were glad when the children were in their beds sleeping. Children starting school automatically took part in the festivities in October to celebrate the victory of the Russian Revolution in 1917. The children gathered in school pairing up in groups of four in rows and proceeded to march through our village of Johannestal saying slogans praising the Oktoberfest. One boy or girl would step out of the line, and hail out, "Eslebe der 1ste Mai". The rest of the children would applaud with three cheers of "Hurray, Hurray, Hurray". The only sort of excitement I felt was when they announced in school that we were to be shown a film (Kino). The film (Kino) was a black and white silent movie. The movie was viewed on the wall, as there were no screens. The movie started with a few minutes of comedy, to try and bring a little laughter amongst the children. The rest of the film would show how much our Leader Stalin loved the children by playing with is own daughter, Svetlana and her few friends. As children we didn't know any better and we enjoyed watching how happy these children in the film were and to see how well and beautiful the girls were dressed compared to ourselves. After the show we would all say to each other in excitement, "Did you see what a fine dress Svetlana was wearing?"

People were not able to purchase anything, we didn't have any money and the only store that was in Johannestal was empty. The regime took everything from the people and kept on coming for more if there was anything available. The people were forced to hide the little bit of wheat or corn that was on hand to them. The horses and cows were already taken away from the families.

Everything was brought into the Collective (Kolchos), which belonged to the communist regime.

At the beginning of the communist regime, the wealthier people who owned more land and bigger more elaborate houses were singled out and were known as, "The Kulaks". Because they owned a better homestead or more land, they were the first ones to be stripped of their possessions by the regime. The only possessions they were left with were the clothes they had on their backs. They were thrown out of their homes. Sometimes whole families were deported to Siberia, Ural or Arkhangels. These families had to sign that they had left of their own free will. A lot of them were taken captive and forced into hard labor camps and sent to Siberia never to return. Some children were left with no parents. The children were either taken in by relatives or sent to orphanages. Some women had to struggle to survive without their husbands.

Under the Communist regime in Russia, everyone paid a high price; all possessions had been taken away. They were stripped of their dignity and pride. Our forefathers had worked so hard to make the steppe productive, working diligently to build homes out of the stones cut at the quarry for their families. Our forefathers were hard driven people. They were driven to achieve more and better for their families, in their adopted land of Russia. The German people were not out to do any harm but were striving for peace. Our forefathers never found that peace, throughout the generations.

Most people disappearances occurred during the late night hours. It was never known where they were taken to or why. Under Communist secrecy, a question was very seldom brought up or spoken about. People were so terrified; they felt ashamed putting the blame upon themselves, as it was considered shameful to be taken away from their family. The fear was so deep rooted among the people, one had to be very wary of what you were saying, and to whom. You never knew who was spying. The slightest word against the Communist Regime, and one would surely be taken away during the night, deported into hard working labour camps. By chance if anyone was lucky to be released from captivity, the experience was kept very quiet.

My father's cousin Anna Zimmermann (nee Roth), husband Johan was very lucky to have been released to come home to his family. No one had been told that Johan had returned. Anna was working in the Collective Brihada, milking cows. These were the same animals that were taken away from the people and put into the Collective. Anna would normally to go work with her feet wrapped in rags, but one day she came to work wearing a pair of men's boots which belonged to her husband. Anna didn't show any kind of excitement or happiness that her husband had returned for fear of the unknown. She kept the secret to herself and avoided any type of conversation.

I remember a specific incident, which occurred with the family of Andreas and Frieda Nadan along with their two small children. Andreas was taken and arrested during the night. Not too long after, the Communist members came to the Nadan home and arrested Frieda without any forewarning. She was ordered and forced to get ready for deportation. As Frieda had very little time she begged for one last wish before being taken from her home. She wanted to play one more song on the organ, which to her surprise they agreed to. The song she played was "Was ich nicht anden kan, nehme ich geduldig an", (What I cannot change, I'll take on with patience). She thought that maybe if the party members had a heart, this song would touch their hearts and allow her stay at home. Frieda Nadan was led away while her two small children, Lina (6 years old) and Edward (4 years old), were sent to an orphanage. Frieda was sentenced to prison for two years, no explanation or reason given. After her release from prison she headed to the orphanage to be reunited with her children. Upon arrival at the orphanage she found her daughter little Lina, now 8 years old, happy to see her mom. It seemed Lina had nicely integrated within the orphanage. She had made friends being too young to understand the circumstances that sent her to the orphanage to begin with. She was happy to go with her mom but had wished some of her little playmates could have gone with her.

Frieda Nadan was anxious to see her little baby boy Edward. Frieda and her little girl, with hands clasped together, headed toward the boys section of the orphanage. Once at the front desk in the boy's section, with grief, handed her son's belongings to Frieda in a bag. The staff at the orphanage told Frieda that her little boy never stopped crying. The little boy was heartbroken and very homesick for his mother.

So many sad things were happening under the Communist Regime. It was a crying shame and the question was "why?" Stalin's Communist regime was responsible for eliminating thousands of lives. Ripping families apart, sending innocent children to orphanages. This was our so-called Great Leader. The children were brainwashed into believing that the leader Joseph Stalin loved and cared for them. In reality he brought suffering, hunger and starvation to thousands of poor innocent children.

No questions were ever asked for fear of their own lives. Everyone was frightened. The silence amongst the people was so deep rooted that they lived from day to day in fear.

When somebody was taken away from their family, they were so afraid. Trying to keep safe, they kept these disappearances undisclosed. All you could see were the tears in their eyes with heavy, broken hearts.

I can still remember well when I was 6 or 7 years

old; my Aunt Rosa lived down the street from us. She came walking over to our house very upset with tears in her eyes. My mother was busy mudding our house, as it still needed a lot of preparation for winter. It was hard work and there was certainly no money to buy supplies. Most of the women worked at the Collective and had to do the work at home while the men worked out on the fields. My mother sensed trouble in Aunt Rosa's eyes. For fear of the worst my mother was scared to ask Aunt Rosa what was wrong. Mother started to wash her hands when Aunt Rosa said to my mother, "Otaria, Can you help me? I just heard that in the very near future my family will surely be deported. To where, God only knows".

My mother asked, "what can we do and are you sure? Aunt Rosa started sobbing and said, " I believe that something is going to happen to my family". My mother asked again, "what can be done"? Aunt Rosa replied, "I'm afraid to work in my home, afraid of having a light on at night and terrified the Communist members will come for us". They would be deported to Siberia like all the rest. She was living in such uncertain times.

My mother told my Aunt Rosa to gather her sewing machine and work in our house after dark. That night Aunt Rosa brought her sewing machine over. My mother covered the small windows to make the house look dark. She made sure that we were in bed so as not to disturb my mother and aunt while sewing.

The two of them spent most of the entire night sewing pieces of flannel together for mittens and also pieces to wrap around the feet to keep warm. I could not fall asleep as the house only had two rooms with a small,

23

little entrance way. I was sleeping in the room where my mother and Aunt Rosa were sewing for hours. I just lay there listening to every word that was spoken pretending asleep. I heard my mother and aunt crying together my eyes also filling with tears. Hearing and seeing them cry broke my little heart. I knew that something was wrong which frightened me. I always feared the worst. As children, at our young ages, we also lived in terror of the unknown. We had to learn quickly in life as to whom we could trust. We learned to be cautious of what was said, as a person never knew who would report or harm your family for a piece of bread. Even our parents were very cautious and careful as to what they were saying in front of the children.

Three days later in the afternoon we noticed that two people whom we called the "communist spies", and who we were all afraid of, were walking down our street. The whole neighborhood was watching and wondering who the next victim would be.

People in the entire village were afraid when the Communist Party members surveyed the village. They were the ones who brought so much misery amongst our German people. Suddenly we noticed that they had turned toward my Aunt Rosa's yard. If something happened the villagers made sure to stay away…they were frightened. I ran toward my Aunt Rosa's house to warn her that the wagon was coming. I yelled, "Aunt Rosa the wagon is coming". In just a few minutes they walked toward my Aunt's door. She opened the door slowly, panic in her eyes. They said to Aunt Rosa the order came from the high command that the whole family must leave at once. Aunt Rosa began to weep, there was no explanation and you wouldn't dare ask any questions for fear what they might do. The two party members, Jelka Chernetzky and Wanja Kolomenchuck entered my Aunt's house and started to take what they wanted. By the time they were finished loading, the house was empty. The one thing that was left behind was Aunt Rosa's bed because Uncle Heinrich was lying under the covers, sick in his bed. When they were taking my aunts few clothes from the house she cried and said to the women calling her by name. "Jelka, please leave me the headscarf, this is all I have left from my mother". Jelka Chernetzky replied, "No, we have orders to take everything."

Uncle Heinrich was bed ridden for weeks with no doctors available to take care of him. He was struggling with serious lung problems, weak, needing a lot of rest.

During this time Aunt Rosa and her two children were being taken from her house into the Collective yard. Standing beside the stone fence, Aunt Rosa and her children were instructed to wait there until her husband could follow them. The plan was to take the entire family away.

Jelka Chernetzky and Wanja Kolomenchuk were two people whom lived among the villagers in Johannestal. The people of Johannestal hadn't the slightest idea that these two people would bring so much destruction to their lives. They were very poor just like the rest of the villagers. Wanja Kolomenchuk was so desperate for food that he would kill village dogs and eat them. Wanja became know among the villagers as the "hund- fresser (the dog eater)". The locals said that even the dogs recognized him and they would run for cover. They smelled his scent and knew they were in danger. It is truly amazing what a human will do to survive. The old saying was, "give a dog a piece of bread and he'll follow you". Wanja and Jelka had secretly become involved in the underground as silent supporters of the Communist Regime. They brought misery to our people and as time went by it became more evident for their support towards the Communist. The people were in shock and disbelief that people who shared and lived in the same community had betrayed them.

Meanwhile the two party members Jelka Chernetzky and Wanja Kolomenchuck put pressure on Uncle Heinrich. They told him repeatedly to get out of bed and accompany his family. They told him that his wife and children were waiting for him. Uncle Heinrich knew that it was not possible for him to move from the bed whatever happened. Jelka and Wanja were getting more aggressive and told Uncle Heinrich that if he did not get out of bed his family will be taken without him. Trying every technique to scare Uncle Heinrich, he prayed in silence that God would be on his side. My Uncle Heinrich said to them, "Wanja, I'm not able to leave my bed, I'm sick and running a fever. Come what may…if I leave my bed I surely will die and I would rather die in my own home".

The two party members, Jelka and Wanja would not go near his bed as they thought that he might have a contagious disease. They finally left him alone, the house now empty and quiet with just the bed on which he was lying on. He prayed that his family would be protected. My Aunt Rosa and the children were still standing at the same spot as instructed where a wagon was waiting to take them away.

It was late summer and the nights were cool. No one was allowed to go near my aunt and her children or to offer any help. It was forbidden to take them in, or even to go inside the Collective's barn, the instructions were to stay. It seemed like a lifetime standing there, waiting, and not knowing what was going to happen next.

My father paced back and forth in our living room. He was helpless, not permitted to be with his sister to give her the emotional support she needed. If you broke the orders you would find yourself in the same situation. The house was being watched and finally the two Communist party members realized that Uncle Heinrich was not going to leave his bed. Now it was close to midnight and they instructed Aunt Rosa to go back to her home with the children. Upon these orders Aunt Rosa and her two children with a small bundle in hand walked toward their home.

My father could not find peace. He was standing outside looking into the darkness and noticed that down the street a woman and children were walking, silently crying…. it was his Sister Rosa. He quickly hid behind the house to meet them. Entering the house where Uncle Heinrich lay in bed, Aunt Rosa was in distress and sobbing. The house was empty, not even a blanket to cover her children for the night. My father retrieved a blanket from our house so that the children could rest and be warm for the night.

A few weeks later, Jelka, the woman that took Aunt Rosa's belongings was wearing the scarf that was taken from my aunt. My aunt couldn't say a word about the scarf. She would be punished.

As my Uncle Heinrich showed signs of improvement he was assigned to do very hard labor for not co-operating with the party members. It didn't take long till he got sick and once again, confined to bed. By trade he was a shoemaker repairing and making shoes. You were not allowed to be self-employed and made to work for the Collective. The workers were divided into groups called the Brihadas. Johannestal was divided into three Brihadas.

Each worker was assigned to his particular workplace. Most of the men worked out in the fields cultivating and seeding with horse and oxen. The women along with the older children had to keep the fields free of weeds hoeing by hand. Your performance was recorded and monitored by men coming out and inspecting to make sure that the job was done appropriately.

The smaller children were brought to the kindergarten where they were given soup for the day. At least it was something to dull the pain of hunger. My brother Gottlieb and I went to kindergarten while my parents went to work on the fields. When my second oldest brother Adolf was born my mother was permitted to stay at home to care of her children. During this time food rations were not given to her. The regimes' saying stated, "No Work, No Eat". My mother was compelled to go back to work in order to help feed the family. The infant was left alone with us smaller children to care for him. You can just imagine how worried my mother was; having to leave her baby home alone with her children. It was up to me to take care of the baby.

Since I was the oldest, but yet still a child, the

burden fell on my shoulders. It was now my responsibility to take care of the baby and my younger brother Gottlieb. Dragging the baby and brother, I went to kindergarten everyday to receive a ladle of soup for each person. After getting the soup I fed the small children making sure to save some soup for my mother, as she was still breast-feeding.

Taking the baby with me, I took the remaining soup out in the field to my mother so she could eat and breast-feed the baby at the same time. As young as I was, I knew that if my mother didn't get any soup, she wouldn't have milk to breastfeed the baby. As a child I carried grown-up responsibilities and knew that my mother also required nourishment.

My parents had to endure long hours of strenuous work. At the end of the workday they received one piece of "Makucha" for their days work. Makucha was the product left over from the sunflowers that were pressed for the oil. The waste was divided among the workers. My parents brought this home for the whole family to eat. My father broke the 12 - 14" round piece into smaller bits with a hammer to share with the family. The pieces were very hard and needed to be chewed to break up. Sometimes my mother soaked the pieces in water to soften the Makucha. This Makucha was meant for feed for the pigs, but because of the shortage of food it was divided amongst the workers to take home to their families to eat. When hunger takes over it's amazing what humans will do for survival.

My mother and Aunt Rosa, with the ground still frozen, would go out to the fields carrying a sack and hatchet looking for dirt mounds where the field mice would store their grain. They chopped the mounds open and gathered the grain into the sacks to take home where the grain heads were rubbed by hand gathering the seeds. After the grain was gathered the seeds got washed, cooked, and were ready to eat. Again we had something for the whole family to eat. This is how our family and many other families struggled to survive.

In the fall, after harvest, it was strictly forbidden to go into the fields to pick the heads of grain from the ground. If you got caught picking the heads of grain you would be punished. When the collective noticed grain on the ground, you would be accused of deliberately leaving the grain out on the fields for the purpose of gathering it later for survival. Many workers were imprisoned for helping themselves to the grain. The people who worked in the collective were ordered out to the fields to pick up any remaining heads of grain and deliver to the collective. This was to go toward the five-year plan, which was always short.

Hunger was widespread, starvation struck daily. The crops had to be delivered to the Government. There was a never-ending five-year plan. The Government demanded this to be filled. The Collective was always short of grain. The communist asked and expected such a high quota that there was nothing left for the people. The people always had hope for better years but were always disappointed.

You could see the happiness when we received several kilo of wheat or corn from the Collective for the working days.

My father was assigned to feed the horses for the

Collective Barn. Each horse was given several ears of corn. The horses were fed better than the people. My father tied the bottom of his pant legs shut with string and when a chance arose he would take a cob from the horses trough and drop it down his pant leg landing down at his ankles, which he brought home for us to eat. Though it was strictly forbidden, luckily he was never caught. Having a large family this helped tremendously.

My Uncle Heinrich grew weaker from lack of food and medication and was no longer able to perform hard work. Uncle Heinrich was forced to dig graves at the cemetery with two other men. It was a full-time job working in the cemetery.

My Uncle Heinrich said that they could not dig the graves fast enough. Burials had to be delayed till the graves were dug. The men were getting weaker and not able to dig the graves that were needed.

Most of the male population disappeared with no trace. Young children were left alone without parents, struggling to survive. Graves were dug with shovels and spades. Many women ended up burying their own children in shallow graves. When the rains were heavy the dirt would wash away, leaving many body parts uncovered. Hungry dogs would drag the corpses around the cemetery. My Uncle Heinrich said it was a terrible sight to see.

One day Uncle Heinrich came home and told his wife Rosa and my dad that he had a horrible day reburying the small body of a child. The corpses were handled as though they were dead animals. Preparation for burial no longer existed; they were merely wrapped in a sheet or blanket and buried. There were no coffins or funeral services.

Hunger and starvation was indescribable and still the Communist Party was still looking for men to condemn. Many who were in hiding eventually were found and sentenced to death, shot or sent to Siberia. The Communists at that time were looking for laborers. The Communist members were also forced to find the required labor quota. The men were sent into the wilderness of Siberia, Ural or other parts of Russia building canals and train tracks over water. Very few of them ever came back, most died of hard labor, hunger and starvation.

4
Fighting For Survival
(1932-1940)

My mother (Otaria Belanov) was an orphaned child at the young age of three. Her mother died while working for the Schorzmann family. She was setting pyramid straw piles at threshing time when she accidentally was pulled by a heavy cord and fell to her death. The Schorzmann family took my mother in as their adopted daughter. The Schorzmann family also had a daughter (Magdalena), and eight sons (Christian, Jakob, John, Gottlieb, Andreas, August, Karl and Emanuel). My mothers' new parents were Katarina and Jakob Schorzmann. Most of her stepbrothers were deported or disappeared later leaving their families behind.

I remember well as a child, when darkness fell, it was time to go to sleep. We had no fuel for the lamps and sitting in the dark was not appealing when hunger was on our minds. We had to accept the situation we were in and the comfort of our beds were relaxing to us. The hunger and craving for food eased as we fell asleep.

It was late in the fall and our families were in their beds sleeping. Near midnight we heard a soft knock at our door. My parents awoke alarmed; I also had awakened and shook with fear, thinking and hoping that our father would not be taken from us.

My mother went silently to the door and asked, "Who is it?" A soft and dim voice answered, "Otaria...open up it's your brother, Andreas." Mother quietly opened the door, meanwhile my father got out of bed very afraid. The first thing my father said to Andreas was, "God Andreas...I hope no one has seen you!" You know they are looking for you and if they discover you in my house they will surely take me away from my family. Uncle Andreas replied, "Karl, I'm certain that no one has seen me. The entire village is dark and it's midnight. Everyone is resting."

In the dark I heard my parents whispering to Uncle Andreas, "we are so glad you are alive and at the same time so afraid that you are here." Uncle Andreas asked my mother and father if they had something to eat. He had not eaten for several days and was so hungry. Uncle Andreas was tired and fatigued. While hiding, his hair had grown long and he was unshaven. My mother said we do not have much to eat just a small piece of mamalika (mixture of corn flour and water cooked to a thick consistency and cut into chunks), which she gave to him. My mother was saving this for my father before he had to go to work in the morning.

As Uncle sat on the stool eating his mamalika my father asked him, "where have you been hiding all this time?" We haven't heard from you for several months. We thought you had been taken away. Uncle Andrew answered, "I was hiding under the straw piles in the fields. During the nights I would search for food in the corn, sunflower fields and in the vineyards. I had found a few grapes but now that fall is approaching I won't be able to survive the winter months without food and shelter. I am forced to take risks to survive."

Uncle Andreas asked my parents how his wife

Bertha and children were. They lived about eight houses down the street from ours. My father said that things were not going very well with them. Bertha has given away the two older children, Amalia and your son Andreas, to another family in hoping that they will have a better chance to survive. In hope of a better life many families chose to give their children away to other families in the larger cities like Odessa and Nikolayev. Most of these children were taken and used as slave labor without being able to attend school and get an education. Their younger two, Olga and Albert are still with Bertha. Bertha is very sick from hunger and can hardly take care of herself.

During the conversation a knock came on the door, which shocked everyone. My father motioned for my Uncle to quickly crawl up to the attic and hide in the chimney. My father proceeded to bed and my mother slowly walked to the door, shaking with fear asking, "who was at the door?" The person on the other side of the door demanded that the door be opened. When the door opened, Jelka Chernezky and Wanja Kolomenchuck were standing there. They asked my mother if she had heard or seen anyone during the night or if someone other than the family was staying in the house. My mother was quick to respond in saying, "No…the family is sleeping. You could come in and look around if you like". They told my mother that if she hears, notices or sees anything to report it immediately. My mother said she would and closed the door as they walked away.

There were many people that spied for the regime. They would spy on families. Many people were brutally beaten and tortured to confess to crimes they had not committed. The regime would then have a reason to punish them.

After my parents went to bed I could hear my parents whispering but couldn't hear what they were saying. My father got out of bed and proceeded up the attic to the hiding place and both my father and Uncle Andreas came down to the living room, which doubled up as a bedroom. Lying in my bed keeping very still and quiet, I heard my Uncle and father speaking clearly. I heard my father tell Andreas that he is afraid of being deported especially if it gets to be known that you were here. Surely my father would be taken from his family. My father was shaking with fear having Uncle Andreas in the house.

My Uncle tried to comfort my dad. He said not to make himself sick with worry. If something should happen to me I will never tell or admit that I was with or have seen you. I'm in God's hands...whatever shall come; I know that I've done nothing wrong.

"I have just one wish", said Uncle Andreas and I hope it can be fulfilled. I would like to see my wife Bertha and children once more before I go back into hiding. If I succeed, with any luck I will work my way toward Odessa. Maybe I can go to some Russian village where I'm not known. There are so many drifters these days and I can possibly find work. Maybe times will change for the better so that we are free and once again be with my family.

My father told Andreas to be very careful. Uncle Andreas said that he had crawled on his knees and stomach to the door and will be leaving the same way. The moon shone in the windows, I could see my dad and Uncle Andreas embracing each other to say good-bye, voices crackling, just as if they knew that would be the last time they would ever see each other again.

Before Uncle Andreas left my parents checked outside to make sure everything was clear. Andreas cautiously walked out of the door with intentions of seeing his wife Bertha and his children. My parents went to bed with heavy hearts and sleep never came as worry and sorrow filled their minds. I couldn't fall asleep either, as I also worried, wiping the tears away from my eyes in the darkness of my home. All was quiet. My parents were whispering, probably worrying about Uncle Andreas and hoping that he will be able to start with a new beginning elsewhere until he could safely return.

A new day was breaking and the sky filled with light. The nights were especially hard as most mishaps occurred during the late evening hours.

Once again it was time for my parents to go to work. Every new day brought more sorrow amongst the villagers. My father along with two other men had to go to the Collective early in the morning to get the horses ready for the days work in the fields. They needed to bring straw and other feed to the barn. Just as my dad went out of the barn door he noticed Aunt Bertha approaching very slowly, her legs swollen. She was carrying a pail in her hand to fetch water.

As she came closer my father approached her with pity. My father said, "good morning", and asked how she was doing? With tearful eyes she glanced up and said, "my children and I are getting weaker by the day and Andreas is gone and I don't know whether he is still alive or not. I haven't heard anything from him." My father stood silent for several seconds and could not say anything as a shocking fear came over him. In his heart he wanted to tell Bertha that Andreas was in our house last night for a short time but not knowing how Bertha would react he did not say anything. It was possible that she would scream out in shock endangering my dad. He knew at that point that something terrible had happened to Andreas because he never made it to see Bertha and the children.

Now my dad's nightmare had came true. He was worried that they may have tortured my Uncle to the point of confessing where he had been the night before and where he had been hiding. Will he say that he was at our house the night before? Is my life at stake? Am I in trouble? He could not say anything; all he could do was wait.

My dad said to Bertha to wait for a moment. My dad went back into the barn ensuring that it was safe and slipped the cobs of corn in Bertha's pail. Now she would have some food for her children to eat. This was a very dangerous thing to do, as this was totally forbidden. A person will do what ever it takes to stay alive.

We were desperately waiting for my father to come home from work at the Collective. Often he would take the food from the horse's trough and brought it home for us to eat that evening. My mother would shell the cobs of corn and boil them. Again we had food for another day as we lived from day to day not knowing where our next meal was coming from. We were thankful to God for still having our father with us. Every time my father would bring food from the barn he put himself in harms way. As poor as we were we considered ourselves lucky, our father was with us. Most men were imprisoned or deported, even worse, dead.

Stalin had the most powerful dictatorship. Collective farming started in 1927-1928 and by 1930 was well established. No one individual owned and land – everyone worked for the state. Thousands of people were led away from their homes and families, only a fraction returned home. In the Ukraine alone, Stalin managed to bring to death thousands and thousands of people from the year 1932-1933 due to starvation and murder.

We lived in constant uncertainty. We weren't sure as to how long it would take before our father would be suddenly taken from us.

People were living worrisome and fearful lives. With the widespread hunger the villagers were getting very weak, people were dying at enormous rates. They were found dead all over in high weeds and old buildings. The death toll was not only in Johannestal. There were many drifters and the homeless in hiding who also met their fate. Slowly the bodies were gathered for burial.

Children went from house to house begging for something to eat. It was heart breaking to see the young children asking for something to eat even if it was a potato peel. There was no one to help; nobody had any food or scraps to give. Many mothers left their young children at home going on foot to different nearby villages looking for food to bring back. The forlorn children would sit beside the house waiting for their mother to return. So many times when their mothers returned they returned empty handed. Again the little children's hopes were shattered. The children once again had to ignore their hunger pains and go to bed hungry, hoping tomorrow maybe; just maybe they would have food tomorrow.

My Aunt Bertha also went by foot, very weak trying to get to the village of Slebucha approximately 20 kilometers from Johannestal. She knew of an uncle in Slebucha that could possibly help the poor children she had left behind. She tried everything she knew to help her children. Aunt Bertha was in no condition to care for her children properly, she herself was nearing the end of her own journey.

Anna and Mina, my fathers' cousins, lived together with their families in a Samelanka (mud house). They had gone out toward the stone quarry to find porcupines to eat. My mother would send me out in the morning to pick green leaves for the soup she planned to make. I would sit on the stonewall in our yard waiting for my father. Whenever he had the chance he would come home during the day hopefully bringing something home to eat. Our minds were consumed with our hunger and where our next meal was coming from.

As I looked down the dusty street two small children were walking and as they came closer I realized that they were Aunt Bertha's children, Albert and Olga. They came into our yard and went straight to our door. Little Olga and Albert stood there pale and hungry. The children begged for my mother to give them something to eat, they were so hungry and their mother had not returned from Slebucha.

My mother said, " children, children, we don't have much either." She told them to go home and bring their bowl and spoon (loshka) and she would give them some leaf soup.

The children continued on home to get their bowls. Bowls were scarce and always shared with the other members of the family. When they came back my mother gave all of us leaf soup. After they had finished, the children stood up and Olga & Albert said "thanks" and walked back home.

I heard my mother say, "My God I hope that Bertha makes it back in time to see her children still alive." The children were near death and no longer had control of their bodily functions. Many children were in the same situation.

A few days later Olga and Albert had not been seen in the village walking the streets. We all knew that Bertha had not made it home yet. The villagers started looking for the two children. They were found dead in their own home. Being so weak they had probably died in their sleep. My Uncle Heinrich was assigned to dig the graves and take the little bodies out and bury them.

Uncle Heinrich placed the small bodies in a kneading trough, which was used to make dough for bread during better times. He covered them with a sheet. My uncle with help from another man carried the children to the graveyard for burial.

Several days later Aunt Bertha was found on the side of the road, very weak and unconsciousness. She was taken to relatives where she was cared for until she regained her strength. Her children had already been buried and Aunt Bertha found out the shocking news about her children's death. It was not possible to delay burial due to the sickness and the spread of disease. Most bodies at this crucial time were simply wrapped in sheets and buried.

The people were frail and lacked the desire to live. Before people died they often had lost their sense of dignity as a human being. It was often said, "Thank God" when someone died. They were now spared from all evil and in God's safe house.

So many mothers' hands were folded in prayer asking God to have pity on the small, innocent children sparing them from the brutality. But God had his own plan and takes only as he wills. It was so sad to see what humans had to go through in their lives, powerless and this was our fate that had befallen us. A better life and improvement was always anticipated but never came.

5
Freedom Returned
(1941-1943)

In 1934 the government promised to improve the living conditions of people in hope for us to live a better life. People were promised more food and hopes were high. It was rumored that on working days you would be provided a ration of wheat at the end of the day. Patiently they waited and the announcement finally came. The workers would receive several kilos of wheat and corn for their day's work.

The more family members that worked the more food rations you received. For example, when both parents worked they received two rations regardless of how many family members they were not working. Over time they were able to store wheat and corn in the attics. The workers were given a sack of wheat from the Collective and it was taken to the mill in Landau, which was approximately 10 kilometers from Johannestal, there the wheat was ground into flour. The flour was brought home where my mother would bake bread. The bread was heavy and dark. I had never seen or tasted white bread in until I arrived in Germany in 1944.

The stored food was used very sparingly for fear of losing these privileges. My parents discussed and planned as to how long these food rations could enable the family to survive.

Everyone tried to erase the horrible past from their thoughts and minds but it was locked in their hearts. No one mentioned the names of our loved ones, who were not so lucky and had died from starvation. You only heard the people saying that the poor souls who went before us were well taken care of. God only knows what lay ahead. The workers believed that if they combined all the power they had and worked harder that maybe the food rations would increase.

In the second movement, the government once again, ordered to continue the food rations for the workers at the end of the working day. After the second ration was given the people thought and hoped that finally all the misery was now over.

Our thoughts were now focused on the better times. People were generally satisfied. They believed the hunger was now over. Poverty was still prevalent with no clothing to wear, or extra blankets. When our clothes needed washing we had no change of clothing so we wrapped ourselves with the blankets on the bed, which were mere rags and waited for our clothes to dry.

The villagers hoped that soon things would improve to the point that possibly one could trade wheat for clothing or, could purchase fabric to sew clothing for their children. The store in Johannestal never carried finished garments. We were only able to purchase fabric, if available. We would stand in line all night, waiting our turn, usually being sold out. Again, we went home empty handed still thankful for the mere rations we had.

Tragically, the opposite occurred. Like a lightning bolt the disturbing news came. Orders were given that all stored food was to be reported and given back to the Collective immediately. There was a shortage of supplies after the harvest and the quota required had not been met. Therefore the villagers had to make up for the shortage by giving up their own rations. The people were shocked and full of fear; no one would survive years of starvation again. In a blink of an eye hunger and starvation was upon us again!

Repeatedly the government requested the required tones of wheat yearly from the villagers to fulfill the five-year plan. Every five years a new contract was written to supply the required quota, which had to be filled. The five-year plan was more important to the government than the thousands of people living in poverty and starvation.

The people could not imagine having to relive their lives as they had endured before and were not freely willing to give up the little bit of wheat they had. They started to hide the wheat by burying the grain in the ground or hiding it in the walls of their homes. Any stowing away of any sort was strongly forbidden.

The Russian party members forcibly went from house to house taking the food away from the families. If grain had been found during the searches, you were arrested and forced to labor camps in Siberia. These were the famine years of 1932 - 1933.

Our family had wheat hidden in the wall just below the window in the kitchen. We had stored about 2 pails of wheat behind the wall. My mother would remove stone blocks from the double walls and would hide the wheat in that space. The hole was covered with cardboard and she then pasted some paper over the hiding spot. If these hiding spots were found you could count on either your mother or father being arrested and taken away never to be heard from again. They were called the traitors against the Regime and The Soviet Union. All the people were at their breaking points.

I was still a child and remember seeing the communist members go from door to door. One of our own villagers by the name of Jelka joined the Communist Regime as an informer. They would convince our own people to spy on the villagers just for a piece of bread.

As the informers came closer to our house I ran to tell my mother, as they were only three houses away. My parents were just having a conversation about the hidden grain. My mother said, "if we give back the small amount of grain that we have we will have nothing left".

My father stood shaking. He said, "I don't know what to do. If I leave the house and they find the hidden grain they will find me and I will be taken." As my mother stood silently tears welting in her eyes, I started to cry.

My mother said to my father (Karl), "As God wills." At this my father didn't now if she meant to keep the grain hidden in hopes that it wouldn't be found or give it freely. I didn't even realize that we had grain hidden until I overheard the conversation. Everyone was very careful what was discussed in front of the children, as you never knew what would accidentally slip out. There was a well-known saying that children and fools always tell the truth.

Without saying a word my mother grabbed the hatchet from under the stool and struck the wall with several blows. I had thought that my mother had gone mad. After several strikes under the kitchen window the hidden wheat poured out of the wall onto the kitchen floor. My father stood in silence with a look as if a huge burden had just been lifted off his shoulders.

At that very moment our front door opened without warning. The feared party members entered the house. Before they had a chance to say anything my mother spoke, calling her by name. "Jelka, we had some grain hidden but we are freely willing to give it back. This is all we have to offer".

My mother and father stood there, relief pumping throughout their veins, watching Jelka and Wanja sweep the grain from the kitchen floor. As they scooped up the wheat my mother pleaded to Jelka to leave just a little wheat for the children. Jelka replied, "No we cannot do that. We are under strict orders from the NKWD (secret police) to fill the quota and the order must be filled." Jelka and Wanja left with grain and before leaving made my parents sign that they had given up the grain freely.
My mother weeping, wiping her face with her apron said to my father, " Now we are in God's hands." But we were thankful that our father was still safe with the family.

We were trying to survive in the most difficult time of our lives. In winter we had no straw to fuel our stoves for heat. My mother would go out to the field in deep snow bundling dry sticks and carrying them home on her back. The dried sticks burned quickly and weren't enough to warm the house. When the temperature got really cold we would gather at my Aunt Rosas' house along with Uncle Heinrich's family each bringing a little bundle of straw to heat the house so we all would have a warm place to sleep.

Our shard experiences brought everyone was close to each other, which helped us to survive. Looking back through my childhood eyes, you never heard children's laughter on the street. There rarely was anything to be happy about. All of us were hungry. When you walked to school and were fortunate to have a little something to eat in your pocket you would dare not tell any one. If it were known that you had something to eat the other children would gang up on you and steal it.

In winter we didn't have warm clothes to wear or shoes on our feet so when the weather was cold we could not go to school. My feet had been frozen many times and often my toes would break open causing painful wounds. To treat these wounds my mother would use a home remedy, which came from a pig's gall bladder. The liquid was applied to the open wounds but took time to heal.

Our shoes were sewn together with rags or pieces of felt. We were not able to wear these homemade so called shoes in wet weather and often had to stay home. On those particular days my mother would tell us to stay in bed so we would stay warm. So we stayed home from school until the weather improved for us to walk to school again. Staying in bed used less energy and therefore we did not get as hungry. There were times we would stay home from school for an entire week till the weather warmed up. We never went to school regularly due to the weather. In those days no one was forced to attend school, but we knew school was important to learn to read and write however many were not interested. Learning was difficult on empty stomachs.

On a regular school day in 1936, we children were shocked and surprised by what had happed. Our German teachers were gone; we never heard or saw them again. Over night Russian speaking teachers replaced them. No one could understand a word of Russian. At the end of the school year the children still hadn't caught on to the Russian language, but the inappropriate words were learned easily. So for the next following school year the Russian speaking children from the neighboring village of Kubraki were ordered to come to Johannestal and go to school with us so we would catch on to Russian faster. The teachers had no choice but to start the children in Grade One no matter what age you were. It took a long time to grasp the language. After a year we slowly caught onto words but were never able to speak fluent Russian. We were not allowed to speak German in class or with our classmates therefore we were quiet and made very slow progress. I am sure that all the other German villages were going through the same or similar experiences.

Practicing any religion at this time was forbidden…what you believed in your heart and mind was kept secret. I had been caught writing a religious song on the back page of my scribbler in school. The teacher had noticed that I was not paying attention in class; my mind was occupied on something else, and not with what was going on in the classroom. The teacher hollered out at me, Anna Karlowna (in Russian your last name was not used but your fathers given name plus "owna" for a girl and "owich" for boys). As I was still jotting the words of the song she called out my name for the second time, "ROTH".

She walked over to my desk and found out I was

writing this song and immediately I was sent to the principles office where I would be lectured and questioned. As I was going to the office I told myself not to say anything so that I wouldn't get in trouble. As I entered the room, scared and shaking, there were two teachers waiting. They were Capitalina Petrowna and Semjan Semjanovich. They questioned me for two hours. They had asked where I had heard this song and if my family sings this song at home or if I had heard it from other family or relatives. I had told them that I can't remember where I had heard this song but I only knew a few words. It was fortunate for myself and family that I didn't have any information for if I had told them the slightest thing we would have been in trouble.

In school one day the subject of religion came up and we were told by the teachers that there was no God. We were told that airplanes were sent up into the sky searching throughout the entire sky, they flew higher than the clouds and there was no God to be found. It was important to the Russian Communist Regime that in the future the children would grow up not believing in God or practice religion.

Even though religion was forbidden, the small groups of people were still holding secret prayer meetings. Fearing that these meetings would be found out the prayers were always held in the dark and in silence trying to make sure that our religion would not be lost or forgotten. If found out the consequences would be heavy.

My father's youngest brother Heinrich was married to "Anna Auch". She had passed away in 1935 with typhoid fever leaving him behind with four children (Lena,

Martha, Amalia and 6-month-old baby boy, Gottlieb). In 1936 Uncle Heinrich married a distant relative Hulda Roth.

Uncle Heinrich's first wife's father, Johan Auch, held most of the secret prayer meetings. He was involved in bringing God's word to the meetings. For holding these meetings he was imprisoned, living in total darkness for years. He was told that if he believed in God and if there is a God than you could pray to your God to show you the light and set you free from jail.

He was released and was returned home to Johannestal an old man, almost blind and not able to walk the streets on his own. He told people how he would pray to God, to be with him during his time behind bars. He said his life was spared through his faith in God. He prayed daily that God walks by my side to permit me to be able to teach God's word in our hearts and soul.

Ours was not the only German settlement living through long years of poverty. In thousands of German settlements hunger and poverty took its toll for families. If we were fortunate to have a few chickens, and if we were able to have supplied feed for the chickens, it was required to report how many chickens we had. According to the amount of chickens one had, an egg quota was to be met for each chicken. This quota was quite high. Many times we had to buy eggs to deliver our quota. Sometimes the Regime picked a property and came and counted your chickens to make sure the Party was not being cheated. If a chicken died, you were at risk of a fine. One had to report and even sometimes bring the dead chicken to prove its demise.

Being able to eat an egg was a very special and rare treat for us. We were able to raise a piglet for our own consumption, and raised it to approximately 100-120 pounds before we butchered it. After butchering the pig, we were required to skin the pig and deliver the pigskin to the government as proof. The livestock had to be accounted for.

We were forced to steal and cheat to have feed for the livestock and for our own survival. Despite all the hurdles we managed to survive.

During the years of 1938 through 1939, we stared to receive larger food rations from the Regime. The people were feeling more positive about life and their future. We were able to raise more chickens for our own use. The people felt a sense of relief that maybe now they had finally overcome the worst things in their lives. Again, mothers were able to provide bread for their families. It was dark and very heavy bread. A mixture of barley, rye and wheat was used. Everyone was relieved to have enough bread, but everything else was scarce. The people had no idea that WW11 was sitting at our doorsteps. We were living such a dark, hidden life, secluded from the outside world. We didn't have access to a newspaper or radio. There was no sort of communication available.

The Russians were using the war as a tool to gain the Germans trust by giving larger food rations. Exporting grain was no longer important, it seemed they were no longer concerned about fulfilling their five-year quota plan.

During the years 1940-1941 the Communist Regime made a last attempt to enroll any available young men in

the army. Everyone was told they had to join the Red
Army. Many boys had been taken a year or so earlier and
no one had heard or seen them ever since.

Now came the time for the 45-50 year old men to be
taken away. My father was among the ones taken away.
These had been the few that had been previously spared
from prison. They were loaded on a wagon with two horses
pulling the wagon, holding a stick or a fork in their hands
for weapons.

The men were not trained for combat let alone
trained to use weapons. These people have never been
allowed to have a weapon in their possession. After the
men had been hauled away only the women and children
were left behind in the village.

With great uncertainty, tears in their eyes, our
mothers waited day after day for their husbands and the
children's fathers to return home. As the days passed no
information about their well being surfaced. It seemed like
they had fallen off the face of the earth.

My mother would often say to us children, " If we
only knew where our father was we would have peace in
our troubled minds". Several weeks passed seeming more
like years since our father had been taken with the rest of
the men. There was no place to obtain any information
and you wouldn't dare ask any questions. We were very
worried about our fathers. We were lost without them.
They were our lifesavers even though we still lived in
poverty.

After a short time had passed by, we heard a sound

in the evening hours that was like thunder in the sky. We thought it must be lightning and bad weather on its way. As daylight broke the sky was clear, not a cloud in the sky. We didn't understand what was happening and caused us little concern.

As night fell the lights in the sky became more visible. The earth would shake as though it was an earthquake. Skies would be lit up at night. Everyone felt uneasy, the lightning came in spurts. The thundering and lightning got heavier which made the sky so bright that if we would have had a newspaper you could read it by the bright light. Sometimes this went on for about 30 minutes and then silence fell. It didn't take long for the thunder and lightning to start again. We were frightened and worried that perhaps our fathers were caught somewhere in the storm. In our minds we were so sure that all the lightning and thunder was just bad weather in the sky. As daylight was approaching, again it was a nice sunny day.

It had been rumored that the Red Army was in training and doing heavy maneuver exercises by Ochakiv near the Black Sea. There were lots of military personnel in Ochakiv, this area was well known for their military exercises.

My mother would stand by the door or by the fence, like many others, waiting for any word or sign about our father. Only God knew where the men were. Orders were for our fathers to be taken away, and help to protect the Russian Army. Our fathers were all very poorly dressed. All they left with were the clothing on their backs, a light jacket, shirt, pants and a cap. Some had sticks in their hands, or pitchforks, when loaded on the wagon and taken away. This was their weaponry.

One morning the women got up after a sleepless night and looked in the southern direction towards Kubraki, our nearest Russian village. The sky was thick and foggy and you couldn't see very far. After a while my mother came into the house calling out our names, " Anna and Gottlieb, come on out if you want to see something." The neighbor lady by the name of Sophie Will was also standing and trying to find an explanation for what they were seeing. Sophie was saying that if you looked in the distance it looked like a train standing there with a long row of cars. None of us could figure out what this could be. I was astonished, as I had never seen a train in my life and besides there weren't any train tracks or station near Johannestal. The nearest train station was approximately 40 kilometer from Johannestal in Berezovka, which was quite a distance from us.

As the fog became clearer you were able to focus better and what we had actually been seeing was a line up of military supply wagons. Things became clearer to us. It must be the Red Army out on their maneuvers. People had come up with various ideas as to the military supply wagons and the thunder and lightning. It was thought that the Red Army was moving toward the Black Sea where they would be continuing their exercises and maneuvers in Ochakiv. No one really knew what this all meant.

On a nice clear day in July 28, 1941, around noon, several motorcycles came rolling down the street ridden by two well-dressed Russian Officers. They stopped several times; speaking fluent Russian questioning some women asking them if any Russian soldiers had passed through.

The women fearfully answered that they had not seen any soldiers around. The soldiers also asked what the name of the village they were in and the women answered, "Johannestal". We thought it a little odd for them not knowing what town they were in.

It was grand for us children to see such beautiful motorcycles and well-dressed officers. Even though we were excited to see these motorcycles we were also scared. The smaller children were hiding behind their mother's aprons and peeking through. We were curious to know what all the commotion was all about. The women gathered and said that they were likely Russian Officers and were looking for soldiers who had run away and hiding to prevent from going to the army. When someone had gone into hiding, our hearts went out to him or her. If they were found they would surely be shot on the spot.

After the officers, on the motorcycles had driven off, the excitement slowly settled down and our thoughts had returned to our loved ones and where they might be.

On that same day close to midday we were surprised to hear voices singing. All the women along with the children ran out of the houses. It seemed like everyone in the village was out on the street. We were all anxious to see what was going on.

We could see well-dressed men marching together singing. Motorcycles accompanied them. As they neared they announced that they were of the German Occupation Forces from Germany and have come to give you the freedom that had been taken from us. We have fought for you our German brothers and sisters and free you from the

Communist Regime.

The German soldiers marched through our village of Johannestal looking splendid and singing, "Heute Gehot uns Deutschland, und Morgan die Ganze Welt". It was heavenly to hear the songs and the whole village was overjoyed. We were so glad to hear our German language again our mother tongue, our language that we'd been deprived of speaking or hearing for so many years.

The German soldiers patiently listened as the villagers expressed the sorrow and pain they had endured. It was a wonderful feeling for the first time to be able to express our hardships freely. With the German Army, we felt full of hope and relieved and felt that freedom would soon be near.

The soldiers comforted the women and children with warmth and understanding. The long lost German people. Oh how we needed this affection, to be able to pour their hearts out to the soldiers. The people felt free. Freedom of speech had not existed for a very long time.

Very emotional and excited the people could hardly believe what had happened. Looked like once again freedom was a reality. Freedom was non-existent under Stalin's dictatorship.

Our mothers started pleading with the soldiers, asking where their husbands and fathers were that had been loaded on wagons and taken toward the east. The German soldiers were very patient and took the time to explain to the women that the German front had progressed far into the east. The soldiers told the villagers that their husbands were probably hiding out and delaying to return home as there were still some Partisans hiding out in areas.

The German soldiers assured the villagers that there was a slim chance that the Russians could of taken them farther east. Thousands of Russian soldiers have already surrendered. In a few days things will calm down and your loved ones will be returning home. These were such comforting words to hear.

Our trust was with the German Army and we believed what we were being told. They assured us that the army was moving into enemy lines and the war will soon be over. They proceeded to tell us that the front line is moving so fast, that the food supply cannot be brought in fast enough. We did not have much to offer but we gave them whatever we could spare. A fair amount of German soldiers were stationed in Johannestal. Until their supplies came we tried to help as much as we could.

We wanted to reward them in any possible way because they were now helping us obtain freedom. Freedom was what we had been yearning for for so long. After several days the news broke that our fathers and husbands were alive and well but in German hands. Our men were now German prisoners of war. The men were detained briefly and would be freed very soon, providing Russian Partisans wouldn't hold them up. We were all overjoyed and happy after receiving the good news. We were hoping that now our fathers would soon be home.

It took approximately a week for our fathers to start returning home. It was a beginning of a new life. Once the men of Johannestal came home, they were full of excitement, and started planning for the future. They hoped that they would get their land back, which had belonged to their ancestors. They had some stumbling blocks to deal with. There was a shortage of machinery and other farm implements. The collective (Brihada) was in possession of the machinery and was not in good condition.

In 1941 the men decided to work together as they had in the Collective but only in much smaller groups. The plans were, in future years to eventually work on their own but still help each other with the shared implements. There was very little machinery in supply, or very run down, so seeding and harvesting was done with the help of others.

The blacksmiths kept very busy working and repairing the machinery. During the Communist rein these implements were broken and run down. Under the Regime the people did not care if the machinery was in good working order as they received little food for the work and the crops belonged to the government. There was nothing to loose.

Changes were happening in the government and now the people were looking forward to the future. In spring of 1942, there was such an excitement amongst the villagers to go out on the fields. Spring arrived early in the vicinity of the Black Sea and seeding started. Most years the crops were seeded in March. Whichever direction you looked the men were working hard seeding the year's crop. The use of horses was required for the cultivation, which was a slow process. The atmosphere amongst the people was good and we all looked forward to the future.

We now had enough bread to eat for the families. The Collectives livestock was divided between the families. Each family now owned a team of horses, cows, chickens and several pigs. We were all content and happy now. You could see more smiles on people's faces. You could see a noticeable difference amongst people. It was a complete turn around in lifestyle. How nice it was to live without fear. It was said in German, "nach dem weinen kommt das lachen, und nach dem regan kommt der sonnen sheine (after the crying comes the laughter, after the rain the sun shines)".

When the German Army had invaded the Russian areas, the livestock had been abandoned. The Russians had planned to take the livestock, which included herds of cattle, horses and pigs toward the East with them. The Germans had moved in too fast forcing the Russian army to leave the livestock behind. The German villagers received permission to gather all of the livestock and bring them back to the village. It was a wonderful feeling, as we had never seen or owned so much livestock ever before, which was all divided amongst the villagers.

I had never seen so much livestock in my life. We had two teams of horses, six milking cows, and six pigs. We already had a few chickens. We could now call this our very own.

Our life was slowly becoming normal again with big promises in sight. The seed was shared for planting in the spring. From seeding to harvest we were not worried or concerned about the times. We had our freedom back.

In Johannestal spring came early and the summers

long. As children we would walk barefoot from March to mid-November. The winters were short which made it easier to cope in the winter months. For the first time, mothers were able to stay home and care for their families. My mother enjoyed her daily work of home cooking, baking kuchen and plachende. My father was doing his work, taking his horse to the well for water. Dad was so proud of his horses; you could find him in the barn grooming the horses with care. In spring it was time to get ready for seeding.

So we all worked together tilling the soil. Women and children would pick and hoe the weeds to keep the fields clean. The next following year with pride everyone worked together to plant and harvest the crops. It would take many years to build up after the destruction from generation after generation. Now we had a nice piece of our own land. We also grew vegetables in our own gardens. We grew plenty of vegetables to last all winter long. We now had enough potatoes, beets, pumpkins, and cabbage. Mother made homemade sour cucumbers, and we also had our own grape vines. Wine was made for those special occasions.

In the year 1942, the men were preparing to go out on the fields to start seeding. The weather was nice and the fields drying up and soon would be time to seed. During the summer, it was announced that a German Pastor was coming to our village. How excited everyone was to hear of the great news. We were excited to be able to celebrate our Evangelical Religion. The ceremonies of Confirmation, Baptism, and Marriages were held on one grand day. Many people were married already, but not through the church. At that time I was 15 years old and registered to be confirmed, and to have the privilege of getting baptized. My parents hadn't' registered early enough; therefore, I was not allowed to be baptized. I needed to have a dress for my conformation, which meant my father had the opportunity to drive with horse and wagon to the big city of Odessa. My mother sent eggs and butter with my dad to go to the bazaar in Odessa and bring some material or something to wear for my Confirmation. My father came back from Odessa with a "ready cut dress in a bag" to sew together. When my mother and my Aunt Rosa laid the pieces of the dress to sew together, some of the pieces were missing. I was disappointed and replied, "There goes my confirmation dress". The only alternative was for me to borrow a dress from someone. The only person my mother and I could think of to borrow a dress from was my Aunt Bertha's daughter Amalie. Amalie had a few nice dresses. My mother asked if she could help me out just for the day of the confirmation. So I was outfitted with a dress, but now I needed a pair of shoes. This was after all a special event. My Aunt Hulda's sister had a pair of shoes to sell, so my mother purchased them. The shoes fit a bit too snug, but I had no other choice. The Confirmation Sunday came, and all of Johannestal was excited looking forward to the event.

That day 300 people were either confirmed, married, or baptized. It was all performed outdoors under the summer sky. On that special day I was happy to dress up in a beautiful dress. I remember the dress was white with big black polka dots, and a black collar. I dreaded having to wear the shoes. By the time the day was over, my feet were aching and swollen. I had noticed that many of the girls and even boys were barefoot and thought that that would have been ok as well. It was a day and a time to remember. Now slowly everything seemed to fall into place. The younger children in our village were starting to befriend each other. We chummed together in groups, and we did a lot of singing. Trying to sing better than the next group was our form of entertainment. In our gatherings the boys were famous for telling jokes.

We were able to spin our own wool to knit sweaters, caps, scarves and stockings. Many evenings were spent with my cousin Amalie Schorzmann; her mother was my Aunt Otilia. My aunt taught me how to embroider. I didn't have the supplies I needed all the time, so my Aunt Otilia usually gave me what I needed.

Young German soldiers, 19-20 years old, were stationed and being trained in Johannestal. Their tents did not have enough available space, so many of the soldiers stayed in the villagers' homes. We had two soldiers, Hugo Seidel and Wilhelm Von Der Heid, stay in our house during the winter of 1943-1944. Very suddenly in the spring of 1944 the military called upon the soldiers, and they were ordered to pack up and move toward the east.

Rumors were flying around that the German army was in trouble. The people did not pay too much attention to these rumors because by now the trust was at a very high level for the German Occupation. The rumors did not stop and heard again that the German Army was retreating, moving back toward the west. We had noticed that some of the military were indeed moving toward the west but we didn't believe it almost to the point of denial. We were told not to worry and to continue preparing for seeding when the time was ready, and that everything was under control. Question after question we were always told just to go out seeding. Surely, if there were any kind of danger the

German Army would let us know. We were very trusting toward the German Army, and depended greatly upon them.

Suddenly on the March 16, 1944, the unexpected happened. We were ordered to leave our village and go towards the west. That evening everyone packed as much of his or her possessions as possible. Covers were pulled over the wagons to shelter the children from the cool nights. My parents packed some essentials of flour, several blankets, and a little bedding. We could not load up as much as we would have liked, as our wagon was not very big, and we needed the room for the four smaller children to ride on the wagon. Early the next morning, March 17/1944 all families were to be ready with wagons loaded and horses hitched, and to meet above the village of Johannestal. The German officers divided us into groups and we were the 17th BK, which meant the 17th district boundary. Before we started moving our wagon, my father walked over toward our house. Standing in the doorway, with both hands touching the door, head bowed, he stood for a minute, slowly lowering his arm and hands, tears in his eyes, bidding farewell to his home.

This little poem represents in my words farewell to my home:

> So leb den wohl du stilles haus
> Ich zieh traurik von dier hinaus
> So leb den wohl, denn ich mus fort
> Noch unbestimt an wechen ort.
>
> So lebe den wohl du schones land
> In dem ich kurze zeit freude fand

Du zogest mich gros und plegest mein
Und niemehr vergese ich dein.

Teuere heimat sei gegrust
Sei gegrust aus weiter ferne
Teuere heimat sei gegrust.

6
The Wagon Train West
(1944)

The one cow that we had, had just given birth that morning, and I was in charge to lead the cow along with us. We left the calf behind. The cow would have plenty of milk for us to drink.

The wagons started moving; you could hear the wheels turning, rumbling on the ground as they turned. You could hear weeping throughout the entire village. My mother rode in the front of the wagon cradling my sister Rosa who was 18 months old in her arms. My mother wrapped the baby in her big shawl. She also supervised the rest of my siblings (Adolf, Hilda and Katharina) who rode on the wagon. My brother Gottlieb and myself walked behind the wagon because there was no room for us. On our journey, I didn't have too much trouble guiding the cow until we almost reached our gathering spot. The cow suddenly started to become very restless, and started fighting for her freedom. I called to Gottlieb to help me with the cow. The both of us could no longer hold onto the rope, and the cow, ran back to the house with the rope still tied around her neck   She wanted her calf, and I ran after her. By the time I reached the barn, the cow was standing in the barn. To my disbelief, there were two German soldiers who had already butchered the newborn calf and were in the process of skinning the calf. I stood crying. One of the German Soldiers told me that they had to butcher the calf, as it would have never survived. Crying, I grabbed the rope and led the cow to where the rest of my family was. The cow was more willing to be led this time. I arrived just in time before the signal was given to start with the wagon train. I tied the cow to the back of the wagon with the rope so she could not run away anymore. We continued to go on leaving our village behind. It was heart breaking, so many tears shed.

We kept on; the trail was slow with many miles to go. The first day we went as far as Rohrbach. As we neared the village we wondered if there would be enough room for so many wagons and people. Entering the village we found it to be abandoned, only a few chickens, dogs and cows walking around aimlessly. The villagers had been evacuated before us, which had been planned so that when we arrived we would have a place to stay for the night. It looked so sad; my thoughts were "how will it be in my village tonight"? If some stay in Johannestal for the night, they must go through the same as we are in the deserted villages. We traveled through Rohrbach, Worms, Bergen, Zibriko, Katzenbach, and through many other villages staying the night. After the long and slow wagon train, we made ourselves at home in the villages. We felt like owners of the village for one night again. In the abandoned cellars we found sour cucumbers, wine in barrels. We butchered some chickens that were left behind during the night. There was not much sleeping or resting for my parents during the night. Nights went by quickly. Every morning we had the same routine, pack the children and head out to the next deserted village. It was a grim feeling to enter uninhabited villages and houses. Our thoughts went back home to our village. We visualized the images of home in our minds. We couldn't stop wondering if our village looked like the many abandoned villages we traveled through. We couldn't help thinking this all was just a bad dream, and thinking that we would be returning home to

Johannestal.

The German Military Personnel accompanied us on our journey. Guiding us the way westward. It was like a big dream in our thoughts. We speculated that going west, out of the danger zone, we would be traveling back to our own homes when safe to go back. Still despite the happenings, we leaned on the German Army for hope and support. We didn't believe that Germany could be loosing the war. We believed that this was only a temporary situation that would be cleared up shortly. Our lives continued day after day towards the west. Each day our situation became more difficult. Soon we were traveling through part of the country of Moldavia. My brother Gottlieb and I were walking behind our wagon day after day, from early morning till the wagon train stopped in the evening. Day by day we were getting more and more tired. It is said in German, "Die longe bringt die last". It meant the longer you walk the heavier the burden will be to carry. Brother Gottlieb and I were singing while walking behind the wagon. Singing made you forget the worries for a while. I thought that maybe that was why the people who worked in the Collective always sang, no matter how desolate they felt.

The following poem was meant for us. This was our life, this was our experience, and this was our way of expressing our feelings. We are the ones in this poem!

Karl Roth Family
Back: Hilda, Gottlieb (Heinrich's son), Anna, Gottlieb, Adolf
Front: Katharina, Rosa, Helene, Otaria, Karl

Otaria and Karl Roth wedding picture (1925)
Top: Otaria Roth, Uncle Heinrich Roth
Bottom: Karl Roth, Katrina Roth

Anna Roth (1941)
Clothes worn were borrowed
from friends and relatives.
This is the first portrait taken
of me. 14 years old.

Anna Roth (1944)
The dress I received
when our family
arrived in
Creglingen, West
Germany

Uncle Heinrich Roth Family
Back: Amalie, Lena, Martha
Front: Herta, Hulda, Katharina (on lap), Heinrich, Lisa,
    Gottlieb

Aunt Hulda Roth, second wife to Uncle Heinrich

Uncle Heinrich drafted to the German Army from Poland

Top: Lena Roth, Rosa Diede
Bottom: Martha Roth, Amalie Roth
Photo taken in Poland

Rudolf and Rosa Diede

Rudolf Diede and
Gottlieb Roth (right)
in the army barracks
in Poland

Labor Camp in Siberia. Rudolf Diede stands in the front
row with bare feet holding an axe over his shoulder.

Rosa Kopp (nee Diede) with her family in the barracks of
Siberia

Otaria Roth stands with Ida Hoffman (right). Ida was the woman who smuggled my cousin Gottlieb across the Russian Zone into West Germany.

My brother Gottlieb Roth was drafted into the German Army at the age of 16 in 1944.

Hilda wearing her Confirmation dress.

Gottlieb/Katarina Roth with their sons Ben and Alvin (sitting)
Wilhelm/Kristina Roth (right) with daughter Louise.

Gottlieb/Katarina Roth
Burstall, Saskatchewan

Gottlieb Roth (1911))
Arrived in the USA in
1909

Wilhelm / Kristina Roth
Homestead in Burstall, Saskatchewan

Wilhelm Roth Family
Back: Emanuel, Gottlieb
Front: Irma, Martha, Kaye, Kristina, Christ, Wilhelm, Louise

Heinrich Diede Family
Top: Rosa, Heinrich, Rosa
Bottom: Berta, Rudolf

Karl Roth Family (1948)
Picture taken before Amalie (left) immigrated to Canada.
The clothing we were wearing was sent to us from relatives
in the USA.

Karl and Otaria Roth standing in front of our
stone house in Creglingen, Germany

My grandmother
Katharina
Schorzmann. She
had adopted my
mother Otaria Roth
(Belanov). In this
era adopted
children were not
given the last name
of adopted parents.

Herta and Lisa Roth
Cousins just recently
contacted after 65
years.

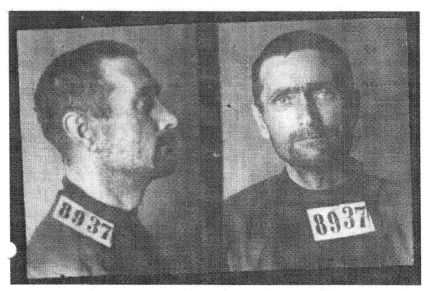

Schorzman Andrey Jakovlevich

Andreas Schorzmann was in hiding from the Russians and appeared at our door late at night. He left to see his wife Bertha but never made it. He was captured.

Waldemar Zimmerman after the mine explosion that left coal imbedded under his skin.

Pflugrath family sent care packages to Germany

Building where refugees stayed before departing to Canada

My parents Karl and Otaria Roth (left) before
leaving for Canada

My family saying farewell to my cousin
Gottlieb before leaving for Canada

Departure from Germany (Sept 1951)
Karl Roth Family seated in the front row

Creglingen, West
Germany

Creglingen, West
Germany

Herrgottskirche,
Creglingen
Every 20 years the
gravesites are re-used.

Karl and Otaria Roth
Creglingen, Germany
(1945)

Karl and Otaria Roth
Medicine Hat, Alberta
(1956)

PERSONENBESCHREIBUNG

Name _Roth_
(bei Frauen auch Geburtsname)
Vornamen _Anna_
(Rufname unterstreichen)

Geburtstag _12.8.1926_
Geburtsort _Johannestal / Ukr._
(Kreis, Land)

Größe in cm und Gestalt _167 kräftig_
Gesichtsform _länglich-rund_
Farbe der Augen _blau_
Unveränderliche Kennzeichen _Fehlen_

Beruf _Hausgehilfin_
Wohnort _Creglingen_
Kreis Mergentheim

Nr. 1078243

Unterschrift des Paßinhabers

Anna Roth

Es wird hiermit bescheinigt, daß der Inhaber die durch das obenstehende Lichtbild dargestellte Person ist und die darunter befindliche Unterschrift eigenhändig vollzogen hat.

Bad Mergentheim, den 7 März 1951

Landratsamt

Im Auftrag:

Nr. 1078243

IMMIGRATION IDENTIFICATION CARD

THIS CARD MUST BE SHOWN TO THE EXAMINING OFFICER AT PORT OF ARRIVAL

Name of passenger _ROTH Anna_

Name of ship _____

Name appears on Return, sheet _27_ line _25_

Medical Examination Stamp   Civil Examination Stamp

LANDED IMMIGRANT

CANADIAN IMMIGRATION
JUN 4 1951
HALIFAX, N.S.

(See back)

87

(Serie 2)

SALÉNREDERIERNA
STOCKHOLM

№ 15

MEALTICKET - ESSENSCHEIN

Anna Roth

Name and Berthnumber

1	2	3	4	5	6	7
1	2	3	4	5	6	7
1	2	3	4	5	6	7

Rederi A.-B. Pulp
Agents:
NORDDEUTSCHER LLOYD
BREMEN / BREMERHAVEN

BERTH CARD

Name *ROTH Anna*   Nom. Roll No. *1139*

Comp.   Bed.-No.

MS. "ANNA SALÉN"

C

ROTH
ANNA

MANIFEST NO. 139

SHEET

LINE

DESTINATION:

RICHMOND. SASK

RE: № 159, Anna ROTH - A.S.S

Total Amount advanced for Transportation Costs			$	285.00
LESS: Ocean Fare	$	138.00		
Rail Fare		61.95		
Meals Enroute		15.50		
Cash Advances		10.00		
Telegraph-Exchange				
Overseas Expenses: As per attached				
Examination Statement		25.15		
Travel Document				
Rail Fare				
Cash Advance				
Bremen Processing Fee		10.00		260.60
Refund of over-payment herewith—			$	24.40

CHAIRMAN   TREASURER

89

Karl Roth Confirmation Certificate

PSALM 23

The LORD is my shepherd;
I shall not want.

He maketh me to lie down in green
pastures: he leadeth me beside
the still waters.

He restoreth my soul: he leadeth me
in the paths of righteousness
for his name's sake.

Yea, though I walk through the valley
of the shadow of death, I
will fear no evil; for thou
art with me; thy rod and thy
staff they comfort me.

Thou preparest a table before me in
the presence of mine enemies;
thou anointest my head with
oil; my cup runneth over.

Surely goodness and mercy shall
follow me all the days of my life:
and I will dwell in the house
of the LORD for ever.

In Memory Of

Karl Roth

December 6, 1901 — November 12, 1979

SERVICES

The Memorial Evangelical Church
Thursday, November 15, 1979, 1:30 p.m.
Rev. A. Roth and Rev. A. Brown

INTERMENT

Hillside Cemetery, Medicine Hat, Alberta

PALLBEARERS

Harvy Roth   Dwayne Roth
Christ Roth   Bruce Fischer
Jeffrey Roth   Robert Kroll

PSALM 23

The Lord is my Shepherd; I shall not want.

He maketh me to lie down in green pastures: He leadeth me beside the still waters.

He restoreth my soul: he leadth me in the paths of righteousness for his name's sake.

Yea, though I walk through the valley of the shadow of death, I will fear no evil: for thou art with me; thy rod and thy staff they comfort me.

Thou preparest a table before me in the presence of mine enemies: thou anointest my head with oil; my cup runneth over.

Surely goodness and mercy shall follow me all the days of my life: and I will dwell in the house of the LORD for ever.

IN MEMORY OF

"OTARIA ROTH"

May 26, 1904 - October 12, 1984

SERVICES
Memorial Evangelical Church
Tuesday, October 16, 1984
1:00 p.m.
Pastor A. Roth

INTERMENT
Hillside Cemetery, Medicine Hat

PALLBEARERS

Jeffrey Roth	Dwayne Roth
Gary Roth	Bruce Fischer
Robert Kroll	Michael Roth

You are cordially invited to be present at the marriage of:

Anne Roth

to:

Fred Fischer

on August 12th, 1955

at 4" o'clock.

at Evangelical Memorial Church Allowance Ave. Medicine Hat.

Rec. Connaught Golf Club

Wedding Invitation

91

Fred Fischer.......my future husband

Fred Fischer Family Homestead
Horsham, Saskatchewan

Anna and Fred Fischer Wedding Party
August 12,1955
Evangelical Memorial Church

Holding my four children
Dale, Melinda, Audrey, Bruce

93

Fred Fischer Family
Horsham, Saskatchewan

On Nov 22/69, Fred tragically passed away
leaving his children and wife behind.

Copy of original letter written in 1929 by Heinrich Roth to his brother Gottlieb in Canada.

Copy of original letter written on February 24,1929 by Karl
Roth to his brother Gottlieb in Canada.

Aus dem Russland sind gezogen,
die verstreute deutsche Leut.
Niemand ging der weg auf Rosen
alle waren sie hier gleich

Freitag fruh im monat marz
in der fruhe jahreszeit musten
wir durch Trubsall zihen wir verstreute deutsche
Deutsche leut.

Angespand und schwehr geladen
stand der wagen vor der tur,
Ach wie ist es uns zuschade
unser Bauernhof bleibt hier.
Und so ging es immer weiter
uber Hugel, Berg und Tall
uber Walder uber Felder
und durch Dorfer manches mahl.
Im gewiter auf dem Felde
sasen wir so manches mahl,
Brot und Wasser war uns bitter,
und wir litten ohne zahl.

Viele Eltren musten weinen,
um ihr heis geiebtes kind
Ach wan werden wir uns wieder sehen
wohl wen der krieg ein ende nimmt.

Und mit diesen schnellen stunden
kam der tot mit schnellen schrit
kleine kinder junge leute
was da lebt, das muste mit.

Zwischen Donau und Carpaten

97

Fluchten wir wochen lag
Wurden geraupt was wir mahl hatten
Foll sorgen undTrauer war gang

Endlich kam ein zug unser richtung.
Nahm uns alle gros und klein
Mit Soldaden schon bewafnet
Fuhren wir in Polen ein.

When we traveled through Moldavia and Romania
we saw how poor these people lived. I could have cried
when I saw this. It reminded me of the life of my own
family. The men were taken to serve in the Romanian
Army, or taken by the Russians and deported. Starving
women and children were all that remained. Feed was
nowhere to be found for our horses. Our mere supply of
food was coming to an end. The roads were very poor
during the springtime and we often became stuck in the
mud. Along the ditches I could see dead prisoners in
ragged clothing and soldiers frozen just barely below the
thin layer of ice. As a young girl it was a horrendous thing
to witness. The men had to pull the wagons one after the
other to free the horses out of the mud. Some places the
wheels of the wagon were half sunk in the mud. We were
not accustomed to traveling through the mountains, hilly
lands and steep valleys. We continued up the mountains
and down the steep muddy roads. The men led one wagon
after the other down the hills by bracing the back wheels
with a long heavy tree trunk holding on each side of the
wagon carefully guiding the wagons down the steep hills.
Sometimes we were so afraid going down steep hills that
the little children were taken out of the wagons to walk
down the hills for fear they would fall from the wagon

edge. As we went through rough areas some would stop and rest gasping for their breath. It looked like they were a bunch of homeless gypsies, sitting and starving and almost dead. There was nothing for them to survive on. Everything was at its worst; it gave me an eerie feeling, with shivers running up and down my spine.

On the way we encountered a donkey standing outside a little town. On the donkey's back, was a big blanket with a side pocket, and in the pocket was a baby, crying. Nobody around. The men were thinking to lead the donkey along with us into the next town, but decided to leave without the child and to report the child in the next town. On arrival in the town, no one was there to report the incident. Everything was boarded shut. We heard that many of the gypsy children were deserted, just left behind to die of starvation. Their parents could not take care of them, so they had to die. So many times I still think of the donkey with the helpless little baby left to die cold and alone.

As weeks went by, our little supplies were running out. There was nowhere to replenish our stock in the poverty stricken countries, there was nothing to receive, and the people suffered everywhere we went. We had nothing. Medication was not provided and people were starting to get sick, especially the very young and the old. My youngest sister Rosa, eighteen months old, also became very ill. There was not a drop of milk for any of the children. We no longer could keep the cow with us, as we had no feed to give her. Leaving us no choice but to abandon her. My mother sat in front of the wagon holding the little one in her arms, protecting her with her shawl that she had over her shoulders to keep herself and Rosa warm.

My father was leading the horses day after day, pulling the wagon with the younger children. My little sister became worse, lifeless at times. My father was walking beside the wagon asking my mother if Rosa, the little one was still alive. My mother would reply with tear filled eyes and nodded her head, meaning, "Yes, she's still alive". I couldn't imagine how my mother felt. You could see the sorrow in her eyes. Her heart pained knowing her little baby that she held close to her heart might die.

We had a small box in front of the wagon containing a few dishes. My father said to mother that if the little one dies, we would use the box, and lay little Rosa in the box. When night would fall we would bury her in the woods. There was no chance to stop during the day. The mud roads were so congested with civilians, but also with military tanks, marching soldiers on foot and big army trucks loaded with German soldiers. The German Army was also taking groups of marching prisoners toward the west. All looked completely drained and worn out. A very young German soldier could hardly walk carrying a pair of army boots strung over his shoulders. He had asked my father if he could hang onto our wagon and walk along. My father agreed, so now there were three of us walking behind the wagon. Holding on made it easier to walk. The young soldier couldn't have been more than 19 or 20 years old. You could see the sorrow in his eyes. Tears rolling down his cheeks, by evening he had to catch up to his troops, he bid thanks to my father for the kindness he was given. He gave me the pair of army boots to wear. I had nothing but rags on my feet. Walking through the mud I had lost one of my rag shoes. I felt privileged to receive something to wear on my feet. I was very happy to receive the pair of army boots, but they were too big for me and I had developed painful blisters on my feet. The army boots were very hard and heavy. In the evening when we came to a stop for the nights rest, my mother handed me a towel and some twine to wrap my soar feet for the next day. Continuing our journey, the next few days, I wore one army boot on one foot and the other foot was wrapped with rags to cover the sores.

We all started losing our strength, nothing to eat and our horses were also showing signs of hunger and weakness. Again we stayed in the forest over night. It was dangerous; we always had to stop in hiding areas because of attacks from the Russians and the bombing sprees. We would always settle for the night in wooded areas. We tried to gather some dried leaves off the ground in the dark for our horses. We were not allowed to show any sign of light, not even a cigarette. If somebody had a cigarette, it was to be smoked in a secluded place. It was strongly forbidden to have any type of light. If a light were spotted, many lives would be in danger.

Our horses were so hungry; father turned them to face the front of the wagon so they could eat the dried leaves that were put in the front. My brother Gottlieb and I always slept under the wagon. We could hear the noise that the horses made gnawing on the wood of the wagon. By morning the horses had eaten two moon shaped circles from the wagon. My mother removed her only ring she owned, and traded it to Moldavian peasants for a sack of straw for the horses. We didn't know how much longer the starving horses would survive. It was nice to be able to sleep on a bit of straw under the wagon.

We were in a strange land, far away from home and

were worried and afraid as to where our travels would take us. How long can we endure this kind of life? How much can we take? We had to continue. Most of the time we were ordered to come to a halt where we would rest for the night; usually hiding in the trees or bushes being careful not to be spotted by the Russian planes (in German they were called the Tiffliger). In the evening, by the time we had reached our resting area, our horses were hungry and exhausted. Once the horses were tied up for the evening my father was responsible for feeding the team. Supplies were scarce; we ate whatever was available. We still had enough bread topped with a layer of fat from the pig we had butchered the night before. With the little bit in our stomachs it was now time to settle down for the evening and hopefully get rest for the journey ahead of us in the morning. My brother Gottlieb and I slept under the wagon where it was somewhat sheltered from the wind and cold. Lying on the ground our clothes and bodies were always damp, if it wasn't the rain it was the drizzling snow. Unfortunately the nice days were far and few between. Even on those nicer days the mud took a long time to dry and traveling was difficult. The temperature would fall below zero, freezing the wheels on the wagons. In the morning the horses would have to pull heavy and hard to get the wheels moving to continue on our journey. As night was drawing closer we had stopped near the Moldavian territory where we stayed in an abandoned building where six or seven wagons full of people spent the night. The women gathered all the provisions available and made soup for everyone to eat. Next morning with the sun rising in the east, daylight breaking, everything was quiet and peaceful. We had thought that maybe the Germans had made progress in the East and maybe we could go back home! We didn't know how far or where we were going, we were exhausted. But the silence didn't last long. Our leader gave the order to proceed and continue traveling on the rough, muddy roads. By nightfall we took shelter amongst the trees in a valley. During the night we woke up to what we thought was thunder. The sky lit up so bright as if it was daylight. What we didn't know was that the fighting was coming closer to our wagon train. We were now all in danger trying to escape and avoid falling into Russian hands with thousands of lives were at stake.

The next day, our wagon train neared the Dniester River in Moldavia. We formed a single line that stretched for miles to prepare to cross. Before we could cross, we received word that during the previous night the Russian soldiers had bombed the bridge killing men, women, and children they had been crossing. We were forced to spend the night on our wagons till daybreak. We now realized what had caused what we thought was thunder and lightning. It was the explosion of the bridge instead. In the morning we were directed to turn in a northwest direction for a few miles to enable us to cross a makeshift pass over the Dniester River.

Arriving close to the Romanian Border with our wagon train, we were ordered to take shelter in a little house over night. The owner of the old mud house was a woman with a child of approximately seven years old. Our women and children lay on the floor to sleep like sardines packed in a can. I was always soft hearted, letting other people come first to find a spot on the floor. To the end, there was no spot left for me. I stood in front of the door, when the lady of the house noticed me. She must have felt sorry for me, and motioned me to come up where she and her daughter were sleeping on top of a flat oven. So I managed to wiggle through the people and nestled myself with them on top of the flat oven. It felt so good. I was so very tired. We did not know the same language, but through gestures and motions we understood each other. The men took turns watching the horses closely as there were hungry wolves that would attack, looking for food by night. The wolves would come down from the mountains at night looking for food in the villages. We could not afford to loose a single horse. We were very dependant on the horses as they were our only source of transportation. Without our horses, we would have been lost, and maybe not even alive. We didn't realize how close the Russians were behind us. We were fleeing for our lives. With no opportunity to bathe or wash clothes we were all infested with lice that was brought on by malnutrition, filth and sickness. The clothes we had on our backs were the ones we left home with. There was no change of clothes. The body lice were so itchy, I scratched and scratched until I had sores. There was no way to rid of the lice as of course the only way to kill them was to boil your clothes and to comb your hair to remove them. We had to move on, as the war was pushing us from behind.

We had been fleeing from March 17, 1944 to the end of June that same year moving towards the Czechoslovakian border. When we arrived at the border with our wagon train we were brought to the freight train station in Tesh. We were told to hand over our wagons and horses to the German army. Two German Army soldiers took each team of horses and wagons and headed toward the east. How far the horses would have to travel, God only knew. Our horses were already to be pitied. They suffered with us day in and day out, traveling along with us, suffering from hunger and yet again subjected to traveling for miles.

At the freight train station in Tesh, we were loaded
on boxcars with approximately 40-50 persons per car. Each
boxcar load was supplied with several loaves of bread to
divide amongst the people. Our future was now dependant
on the train to move us forward. Many times the train
stopped to avoid air attacks from the Russian Air Force.
We were now entering the country of Poland. Upon our
arrival we were transferred to camps and barracks at the
City of Kruszwica. Like animals we got moved to a large
open facility, which had two separate entrances. The men
and boys formed a line at one entrance and the women and
girls formed another line at the other entrance where we
were told that we would have to be deloused. Once in the
building, we were ordered to strip. There we stood feeling
degraded, stripped of our dignity young and old alike. As
the line moves forward our clothes that we were carrying
were placed on a conveyor belt and went through the
delousing process. Entering the next room our clothes
were waiting for us and we could get dressed. We then had
a quick medical where the doctor recorded the results from
checking our eyes, ears, blood pressure, age and height.
From there we were escorted to the barracks. Inside the
barracks there were bunk beds two to three tiers high. The
beds were layered with a thin covering of straw. Bags were
filled with straw and used as mattresses. The barracks
didn't have any facilities to shower or bathe, or even to
wash your hair. The barracks were also infested with lice
and bedbugs. It was a miracle that my sister Rosa was still
alive being so very sick and full of lice. After the doctor had
given her the medical exam, she was immediately taken to
the hospital in Inowroclaw (Hohensalza), Poland. Being
malnourished, she had grown very long thin hair on her

back. At the hospital she was given great care with medication available. The nurses loved her, where she was nursed back to a normal healthy child. Little Rosa was the cutest little baby, with her blonde hair. The German's called her "eine rein deutsche (a pure German)". Occasionally my mother had the opportunity to go to Inowroclaw where she had the chance to visit Rosa. My mother would find Rosa in the arms of one of the nurses. Rosa didn't seem to be missing her mother at all. She loved her caregivers and they loved her back, showering her with lots of hugs and kisses.

We struggled in the barracks. After a week my brother Adolf became very weak as the bedbugs were sucking the blood from his body nightly. He was so week he could no longer walk. A doctor came around and had given Adolf medication and a salve to rub on his body at night to deter the bugs from biting. At night when I would lay down I could feel them crawling over my face. I was fortunate that they didn't bite me. The doctor had explained that the bugs don't attack everyone just going for a certain blood type. Everyday a big cast-iron kettle filled with water was brought to a boil, and everyone's clothing was boiled to kill the lice. One could never be free of lice, living in filthy conditions. After the clothing was immersed in the boiling water, it was let to cool down. As my mother removed the clothing from the big cast iron kettle, you could see a film of dead lice floating on top of the water.

Every morning a truck stopped by the barracks and all the young girls and boys were loaded up and taken to a large farm where we were all given a hoe and instructed to weed the beet fields. We would work from the morning till about four o'clock in the afternoon and then transported back to the barracks. In return for the days work, the farmer supplied the camp with beets and potatoes to make soup.

After a few weeks of staying in the camp we were all ordered out of the camp and preceded to the market square for an announcement. We all gathered waiting, curious as to what the big secret was. Over the loudspeakers, the announcement came. There had been an assassination attempt made on the "Fuhrer, Adolf Hitler". The broadcast continued to say that the assassination attempt had not been successful and whoever was responsible had not yet been found. Our Fuhrer was alive and not hurt. After the news we all walked back to the barracks. With the attempt on Hitler's life our trust level in our Fuhrer weakened. He was supposed to be the strong one and to lead us thorough these hard times. We were scared of the unknown, and now we knew there was no returning back to our home. We had nowhere to go.

7
Creglingen, Our New Home
(1944-1951)

During Hitler's rule, arrangements were made
with the Russian government (1939-1940) to relocate all the
German's from Besarabia to the west. These German
Besarabian people were brought to settle in Poland and the
Polish people were stripped of their own land. The
German from Besarabia were settling on Polish farmland.
The Polish people now had to work for the new
landowners....many times on their own land that they had
once owned.

The German authorities started to relocate the
people from the camps into villages or out in the country
to work for the German farmers in Poland. The families
had no choice or say where they would be sent. Many
families were separated from each other, and each family
went to a different destination, wherever the German Army
had found room for them.

My Aunt Rosa Diede and husband Heinrich with
their children received orders to pack up and were
transported out of the camp. At the Kruszwica train
station they had to sit on top of a boxcar loaded full of
coal. As the train slowly started to roll puffing away big
clouds of black smoke, we could hear Aunt Rosa calling
and weeping out to her brother, "KARL – KARL- KARL".
We stood and watched the train rolling down the tracks,
waving goodbye till the train left our sight. A few days later
my dad's youngest brother, Heinrich with his family, was
ordered to be taken from the camp for an unknown

location. All were scattered in the Polish area. My father applied to go along with his brothers or at least to be able to live near by. We were not allowed to go, which unbeknownst to us was a blessing and saving grace. This was the last time that my family saw any living relatives.

After a week went by our family was notified that we were to be moved out of the camp very soon. My parents feared that my little sister Rosa would be placed in an orphanage and we would never see her again. My parents immediately went by train to Hohansalza Hospital to pick up my little sister Rosa so she would be with us when the time came for us to leave the camp. The trip to Hohensalsa from Kruszwica was a short trip by train. My mother went to the hospital stretching her arms out for Rosa, but she shied away. One of the nurses was holding Rosa, and as my mother came closer to the nurse to take Rosa, little Rosa swung away; she didn't want to go with her mother. Rosa had quite comfortably adjusted to her surroundings and to the nurses. My mother had to pry Rosa away from the nurse. When my mother was leaving with Rosa, she cried out for the nurses, with her little outstretched arms toward them. The nurses followed my mother with Rosa in her arms to the door of the hospital. I'm sure the nurses had to hold back their own tears to see Rosa leaving. They had become very attached to her. My parents came back to the barracks with Rosa. We were told how Rosa had cried for the nurses, and cried all the way to the train station. My parents were in peace that Rosa had recovered during her stay in hospital. We were all now together as a family.

Two days later we received orders to get ready, we were loaded on a passenger train. We never knew where our destination would be. My father was hoping to settle in the vicinity of his brother and sister. The direction of our journey went westward, deeper into Germany. Today looking back, it was our luck that my family didn't have to go through the misery that some of our relatives had when transported to Siberia.

In the middle of July we had finally ended up in Schwabisch Gmund another camp for displaced and homeless people. It was just a temporary shelter. The shelters were set up in Central Germany. Germany was shrinking as the war was closing in. Germany had a hard time with the ongoing war and still no future ahead of us.

The building we were staying in were long and housed so many people from different nationalities. We felt helpless with frequent bomb alarms and military activity going on. When the alarms sounded we had to take cover in the underground bunkers till they stopped. We spent more time in underground bunkers than we did above ground. Sometimes the sirens kept us going to the bunkers two or three times during the night. We were in Schwabisch Gmund for approximately 1-1 1/2 weeks. It seemed a long time to us. The food was sparse. We received a baked potato for each member of the family, and nothing else. The potatoes were already rotting under the peels, but we ate them anyway, we were that hungry. We were hoping to get out of the camp to find peace and freedom. We could still hear the rumbling of bombs and gunfire day and night.

Thousands of Germans were arriving in the camp daily from the eastern part of the country. There was no place for the people to settle, no refuge. While in the camps, business owners came to the camps looking for workers. All the young men were in the military and all there were left to do the hard labor were elderly men, women and young children.

The authorities from the camp took our entire family into the main office at the camp where we were questioned. We were asked what kind of work we were able to do. Their records said my parents were skilled farmers. They asked me if I would be able to milk cows. We tried hard to satisfy their questions. We wanted to get out of the dangerous camp. Some people were taken out to work in factories. Working in the factories was also dangerous as there were still many bomb attacks in the cities. My entire family was assigned to a small sawmill business owner. Wilhelm Kerndner. He picked us up from the camp, and accompanied us on the train from Schwabisch Gmund. We all traveled together by train, changing trains once in Mergdendheim. August 1st we landed in a small train station in the town of Creglingen district KR (Kreis) Bad Mergantheim. We were all full of enthusiasm, wondering what lay ahead for us.

A very small house was arranged for our family to live in. There were two small rooms and a small kitchen for the nine of us. Unknown to me, my mother was expecting another child. I didn't have the slightest idea that mother was with child. Back in those days, a pregnant woman would try to hide her pregnancy. Women felt embarrassed about their protruding tummies; it was as if they were ashamed of their body's appearance.

The day we landed in Creglingen was also my brother Gottliebs birthday. He had just turned 16 years old.

111

In the town of Creglingen I was taken to a small farmer to work. My employer was Georg Balbach. I had so much to learn in tilling the land with a plow and cow. It was a big change for me. I had to cut green alfalfa with a scythe and bring the alfalfa home for the cows. The cows never came out of the barns for grazing as he only had a few acres of land. There were no pastures for grazing. Once the cows were fed I milked the cows for their milk. The days were very long and I had to work very hard.

My father and my brother Gottlieb worked at the sawmill cutting trees into boards. The three of us were working hard to support the family. My pay was low; I was given 25 DM a month. All my earnings were given to my parents. Food was purchased with ration cards. Every person received a few grams of food per month with these ration cards. We had to be very thrifty with our purchases. Although the war was still going on we felt more secure having jobs and a roof over our heads. Even with the scarcities we had our rations of food to eat. My family was used to living on food rations. We knew how to live frugally; we had been through this before back in our birth land Ukraine.

In September of 1944, the small towns Burgemeister's (mayor) son was to be drafted. This young man turned nineteen years old, and received his calling to join the army. The Burgemeister belonged to the Nazi Party and his son went into hiding. The Burgemeister had to fill the Quota for Creglingen, so he called my brother to the army in place of his own son. The Burgemeister knew we were the first family that had arrived in Creglingen, and we were scared, never complaining, trying to fit in as the new Germans. My brother Gottlieb was drafted into the

Hitler Youth Force. He had just turned 16 one month earlier, much too young to be in the army but he was taken away anyway. He was taken to a training camp in Czechoslovakia in the vicinity of Budwiess. Now with one person missing to help provide for the family, we all had to work extra hard. I was a young girl working like a slave. My young life was full of worries and concerns for our family's future. I could never visualize a peaceful and a happy time in the future. All I knew was unhappy times. Never a smile or a happy hour came from our hearts. The only things in my life were thoughts of survival for our family. I had no such thing as a teen life. There was no chance for a future for us homeless and displaced people. We hoped and prayed to maintain our health so we were able to work and provide for our family.

My youngest sister Helene was born October 31, 1944. I was shocked and angered as I received the news of the new arrival. This meant yet another mouth to feed when we hardly had enough for the family we had. I couldn't find the words to describe the way I was feeling. Feelings of hurt, anger, and despair. I was really struggling to accept the birth of my sister but I had to accept the fact and keep on working for my family. With many tears and prayers I found comfort and accepted the situation my family was in. The little one now also was part of our family in spite of all that we had to face. Looking back at that time period, just turning 18 years old on August 12, I felt embarrassed that my mother would have still had a child at forty years old, and with the war still going on. It all turned out for the better, as we now received another ration. It meant several more grams of ratios for our family.

Germany had a heavy burden to bear in the middle

of the war, a small country, and thousands of transients with so many cities and towns lying in ruins. Hundreds of children arrived daily by train from the bombed cities and brought to the rural areas for safety. Some families had taken several children in their homes and provided the essentials until they could return to their own homes or sent to orphanages. They needed shelter and food and to be taken care of.

Things didn't look promising and didn't give us a positive feeling. We were powerless as to the outcome of our lives. Day by day we had to go on with our work.

Our wishes were that the terrible war would come to an end and we could sleep and live in peace once more. Day after day more homeless people by the train full arrived. The bombing took its toll, especially in the larger cities. The frustration and constant exhaustion among the people was in every direction like hitting a dead wall. Germany was surrounded by the allies from all sides; there was nowhere for them to go. The German people had lost all confidence in winning the war. The news was not broadcast to the public. Life went on through speculation alone.

8
Germany Defeated
(1945)

Finally on May 9, 1945 it was official, Germany
announced they had surrendered. The war was finally over.
The German people were glad, and relieved the war had
ended. It was hard accepting the surrender of the German
Army and the loss of so many lives. People still
remembered Adolf Hitler saying, "Heute gehort uns
Deutschland und morgen die genze welt"; "We shall never
surrender". We now had to face reality and wait and see
what the future would bring for all of us.

Germany now a shattered country had the enormous
task of rebuilding the country. Survivors searched for
loved ones scattered throughout different countries during
the war. Some were found dead; some were reunited with
family and some never to be heard or seen again. The
German Red Cross was involved in searching for the
missing persons. There was hardly a family that didn't have
a family member whom they were searching for. Our
family was in the same situation. We didn't know where
our relatives were. My Father was working with The Red
Cross in locating his brother Heinrich and his sister Rosa
who were left behind in Poland. Also my brother Gottlieb
was missing as a German soldier. There were many
worrisome and sleepless nights, but we never gave up hope
that one day we all would be reunited. We had to have
hope and patience that the government would straighten
out the turmoil left behind from the war. The Red Cross
was working with prison camps as well with civilians in
search of missing persons.

Approximately one year after the war had ended, we received good news from The Red Cross. They had located my brother Gottlieb that he was alive and was being held as a prisoner of war by the French Army. It was stated that Gottlieb Roth was captured on April 14, 1945 in the heart of Germany in Frankfurt AM Rhine River. Gottlieb was taken to a camp, which was located on German soil. The camp was surrounded with a barbwire fence patrolled by French Military. Gottlieb was 16 years old and the youngest prisoner of the 20,000 prisoners captured. From this camp the prisoners were transported with open military trucks and taken towards Strasburg, which was occupied by the French. Upon arrival the prisoners including my brother were ordered to march through the main street of Strasburg towards the train station. Once aboard the train station Gottlieb landed in a prison camp in France. The forwarding address given to us was from the Red Cross was as follows:

> Gottlieb Roth
> Gefangene N – 901-801
> Lager 221
> Lager – Bezeichnung
> Comeiles in Paris S/O
> (Frank Reich)

From the camp, Gottlieb was taken to work for a French farmer. When he arrived at the farm, there were already three German prisoners working for the farmer. One of the first questions one of the prisoners asked Gottlieb was, "Have you got lice?" He replied jokingly, "I have no lice, they have me! I'm just full of them. Haven't seen one of us yet without lice?" Gottlieb's clothing was stripped off his body and a potato bag was wrapped around him. Immersing them in boiling water killing the lice disinfected his clothing. The boiling water had ruined his clothing so he had to revert to using potato sacks for clothing. After several potato sacks had been worn out, the prisoners demanded clothing from the farmer. They stated that they would not work if he didn't meet their demands and supply the clothes. The prisoners heard that clothing was to be supplied by the Red Cross for the German prisoners. The farmer had picked up the clothing and sold the items on the black market for his own benefit. The young prisoners of war demanded they would not come out of the hut until the farmer would bring them each a pair of pants to wear. Within a few hours the prisoners were supplied with the pants they had requested. Working in the hot sun without shirts, they decided to demand shirts and underwear or they wouldn't work. These items were also supplied. After working there for two years, my brother was transferred to another camp in Elsas Lotringen by Metz, which is also in France. From there he was taken to work in a large greenhouse, which was German owned.

What a comfort and relief for my parents knowing their son was alive. My parents were hoping and praying to receive some word from Gottlieb. The prisoners of war were not allowed to write letters for a period of one year. The mail during this time was very slow. Day after day my mother would wait for a letter to arrive. I remember the first letter we received from my brother Gottlieb while in France. We were all so happy, sitting and crying tears of joy. We were overjoyed that he didn't fall into the hands of the Russians, where surely he would have met his fate. He was released after 3 ½ years in prison in December of 1948. He came back home to his family in Creglingen. I can still recall how happy my parents were when my brother made it home. He also was introduced to a new baby sister Helene, whom he had never met. She was born October 31 a month after Gottlieb was drafted.

Gottlieb started working with my father in the sawmill. We tried hard to fit in with the German people. We wanted to belong. We became accustomed to our new surroundings. Trusting so we would not feel like strangers. We made every effort to accept everything that came our way. We knew we were Germans, but we were looked upon as Black Sea Germans, born in the Ukraine. Germany was a strange country to us. Germany was our Ancestral birthplace, the origin of our forefathers several hundred years ago.

It was said that with a stick in your hand you are migrating from Germany to Russia. And the time will come with the stick in your hand you will be forced to leave Russia and return home to Germany.

The German-Russian people who had lived during this period and experienced the hard times remember the saying, "Yes, the prophecy was fulfilled".

The Germany born Germans made us feel unwanted and unwelcome. We were looked upon as Russians and not Germans. Feelings of depression, no self worth and a feeling of wanting to belong overwhelmed us. We were not able to return to our home country. We were not at fault for all the destruction, poverty and misery during the war and what we had experienced. Nothing could have been worse than for us to return to our sad past in Russia.

My father was still troubled as to where his brother and sister were. He constantly kept in contact with the Red Cross. In time we were notified that my Uncle Heinrich Roth had been wounded and was in a hospital. In the meantime he was released and found out where his family was. He tried to join his family. They had escaped from Poland in January 1945 and landed in the northern part of Germany. During their escape two of the children's feet were very badly frozen. They were hospitalized for treatment, and my Aunt Hulda with her other children carried on with one horse and wagon.

This was the last time we had any contact with any of my father's immediate family. My father wrote letter after letter, but had no response. He was full of despair, but he never gave up. He continued to write his letters. Finally after many letters, a reply was received from a farmer from the Northern part of Germany.

Dear Mr. Roth,
I am sorry to inform you with some sad news. This family you are writing to is no longer here. The father of the family came here from the hospital. Two days later during the night, the Russians came and took the family away on a wagon. I do not know where they were taken. I spoke to your brother Heinrich and he was very sad that several of his children were lost. He wanted to try to find them through the Red Cross. Mr. Roth I am sorry, that is all I can tell you about your brother Heinrich.

From that moment on, my father knew right away what had happened. He knew that his brother had no

119

chance to begin searching for the missing children. Uncle Heinrich's had made all efforts to finding his children, but in the two days, he was powerless.

My father had begun his efforts in searching for his brothers' missing children, Amalie and Gottlieb. My father thought that he would do what he could for his brother Heinrich. My father took the load on his shoulders, which his brother was not able to do. In the event we would receive information about the two children, we were hoping that we would be able to inform Uncle Heinrich that his children were safe. After searching and writing back and forth with the Red Cross, we received word that the two children, Amalie and Gottlieb were located in the Russian zone of East Germany. After Amalie and Gottlieb were released from the hospital, a German family had taken Amalie in and Gottlieb to an orphanage as it was presumed that they had no family left. Through the Red Cross we were able to make contact with the children. We were not able to cross the border to the east and bring the children across the Russian occupied zone. It was too dangerous as people were afraid of ending up in the Russian's hands or getting shot. Many tried to escape from the Eastern Zone and were shot to their deaths by the Russians while trying to cross the border.

Still working for the Balbach family, working late hours, I would go check in on my family. The Americans had set a curfew for 8 P.M. No one was allowed outside. Because my workday did not end till after 8 P.M. I couldn't go to see my family. After a few days I took the chance and headed towards where my family was living and got stopped by a soldier who was patrolling the area. Crying and very scared I tried to explain to him that I was just going to see my family. To my surprise he started speaking to me in his broken German and told me to go up to the area that was not patrolled. I was very lucky as I could have been in very serious trouble.

In the fall of 1946, a young lady by the name of Inge, with whom Amalie was staying was able to secretly cross the border into West Germany with Amalie. We were thankful to Miss Inge for bringing Amalie to us. She was able to bring Amalie across the border and reunite my cousin with our family. Miss Inge wanted to remain in West Germany. She had relatives and friends there. She stayed at our home briefly, and soon decided to travel to where her friends and family lived. We were glad to have one of Uncle Heinrich's children safe with us. Now we still needed to get my cousin Gottlieb out of the orphanage. My father was now worried and concerned as to how he could possibly bring the young child out of the orphanage. We had to try to bring him across the Russian occupied border to Western Germany. The biggest part of West Germany was occupied by the American, British and French troops. The Americans occupied the west part of Germany, where we lived.

We had become acquainted with a lady by the name Ida Hoffman. She moved from the small farming town with her children to the small city of Creglingen where we lived. Her family was also a Russian-German. Ida's husband was missing in the war, never to be heard of again. Ida went to a location close to the Russian border to meet a dear friend of hers. Her lady friend was living in the Russian zone and was involved with a Russian officer. For this reason she was able to cross the border and visit with Ida and by coincidence, during one of their discussions, Ida found the location of the orphanage where Gottlieb at. It happened to be very close by. Ida discussed with her lady friend about the child, Gottlieb, and how my father wished to retrieve the boy out of the orphanage.

By now Ida was a very good friend to my parents. Every time Ida went away, my parents took care of her children until she returned. Ida approached her lady friend to see if it would be possible to bring little Gottlieb across the border with her. This lady agreed with a condition that a supply of food be exchanged. Ida was excited now to bring the wonderful news to my parents. Coffee was one of the supplies that were used to bribe the Russian officers to find information. Ida's lady friend was also a Russian-German and was very good in speaking the Russian language, which was very helpful. Ida was telling my parents that her lady friend was waiting for the perfect opportunity for her to escape.

Ida returned from her visit and told of the exchange agreement for Gottlieb. Food was scarce after the war, which made money useless since there was hardly any food to purchase. During the current year, our family was receiving care packages through the Church Missions from the USA. We also received some packages from our relatives from North Dakota, USA. These packages were a Godsend to our family. We were in much need of food and clothing.

My parents had decided to save some food packages to send along with Ida. Whenever Ida decided to make a trip to the East, we sent along these supplies to smuggle Gottlieb across the border. The first few trips, nothing happened. We never gave up. Our father was telling us that we must do everything in our power before it gets worse or we will lose our cousin Gottlieb forever. Another month went by. My father would not rest until his mission was fulfilled. Our family was waiting day after day for any package of supplies being sent to us. Ida also had to be paid with food provisions; she was a mother of four children. Again Ida took the journey to the East into the Russian zone to meet with her lady friend.

After this journey back to Western Germany, Ida arrived at our door holding little Gottlieb's hand. Our whole family was overjoyed and very happy, we were all in tears. My father said that it was worth the many worries and sleepless nights for Gottlieb's return. The family was now complete and happy that another goal was accomplished. Our worries never stopped, one problem lead to another, as there were so many of our relatives missing. My father was not at peace. He was striving for answers as to the where his brother, sister and their families were. My father would have been so happy to be able to embrace his brother Heinrich and to let him know that his two children were safe.

We were horrified to find that little Gottlieb's front part of both of his little feet were amputated because they were frozen during the flight to North Germany. He had learned to walk on his heels. We were concerned about his future. Would he be able to work and how would he ever be able to support himself. We were now a family with eleven persons. We made due with what we had. We worked together and all pitched in to support the family.

My father's only sister with family were somewhere in the troubled world. We were hearing hard breaking news about the Russian occupation in the East Germany and Poland. How brutal the German people as well as our Germans from Russia were mistreated. Their suffering was inhumane and horrifying.

After several years of searching with the help of the Red Cross we were beginning to receive messages or letters from our loved ones in Siberia. It took some time till our people were able to correspond by mail. The first letter my father received was from Heinrich's wife Hulda. She wrote that in the middle of the night her family was taken away from North Germany by the Russians and taken to camps in Poland. The Russians took Uncle Heinrich away from his family to do work for the Russians. After a short stay at camp, Hulda was loaded with her children into a freight transport wagon. The wagon was packed with many people. From there they faced a long journey to Siberia. It was already winter. They were housed in old barracks. It was bitterly cold with little to eat and no warm clothing. At times they had to walk up to 3 km in the forest through deep snow to their workstations. Their jobs were to cut down trees in the forest. They left the barracks early in the morning while still dark and return back to the barracks by evening in the dark. Most of the time they slept in their clothes, as that was the only way to have them halfway dry by the time they had to go to work the next morning. It was hard to get a good night sleep in the barracks, it was cold, and it took hours till one warmed up.

My cousin Martha, my Uncle Heinrich's daughter, was taken to work on the train track in Siberia. She worked very hard lifting railway ties. Martha obtained internal injuries from heavy lifting and died at the age of fourteen years old. One cannot imagine the pain that this girl must have gone through. What a shame for the loss of such a young life, and the cruelty endured.

Hulda wrote that Uncle Heinrich was finally released from his Russian captors, and was finally able to locate his family in Siberia. He was a very sick man, too weak to work, with very little to eat. Heinrich asked his daughter Lina to come with him to go to a bazaar (market) to get something to eat. He was hunger driven and being so weak he fell and was injured internally, causing his death. So sad he had to die without knowing where his missing children were. Uncle Heinrich died two months after his daughter Martha. Uncle Heinrich was buried beside his daughter Martha in the Siberian wilderness, beside a big tree in a shallow grave; a stick bound with rope made into a cross was the marker for the gravesite. Aunt Hulda said that they were very poor. With help, they buried daughter and husband; no funeral; no casket. In time the stick cross disappeared and the burial site was never found again. The children of Uncle Heinrich said, "Dad, rest in peace". She continued to write that they were getting chased out to work like a bunch of animals. All you heard was "Daway, Daway", meaning "Come on, Come on". They were treated as though they were P.O.W.'s.

Through the Red Cross we had finally found where my Aunt Rosa and Uncle Heinrich were located in Siberia. We received terrible news from my cousin Rosa Diede (my father's sister's daughter). She wrote that both her parents had died close together only a few months apart from starvation in Siberia in the year 1945. Rosa had to help dig her mother and father's graves. Rosa and her siblings stood by their parents' graves saying their good-byes to them. Rosa at that time was 17 years old. She wrote to my father saying that she had a big burden to carry. She could not see how she would be able to manage taking care of her siblings. Her brother Rudolf, 14 years old, and her sister Berta being 10 years old. She was worried as to how they would survive without their parents. Both Rosa and Rudolf were working in the forest felling trees. Berta was left behind in the barracks, waiting for her brother and sister to come back from work day after day. They missed their parents so much. She wrote to my father; "Uncle Karl, my mother was heartbroken and cried many times. My mother missed her brothers Karl and Heinrich. Today my parents would be so thankful, only to know that you are OK and alive. It was her only wish to be reunited".

My father was glad to hear that at least some of our loved ones were alive, however, they were in great need. They informed us of the terrible situation, but there was nothing we could do to help.

My father wanted so much to help, but our family was also struggling in Germany. We didn't have much either. The only thing that helped to save our lives was the care packages we were receiving from America. My father said if we would have the chance to help we could spare a package and send it along to Rosa, but we had no money to send the package. After the war the money had no value. Germany now was in a recession. The package would have not even arrived, as the Russians would have taken it away. The borders were not settled. Germany was surrounded by all the major powers, Russia, France, England and the Americans. The food was very sparse only given out with ration cards.

Our family of eleven people appreciated every little

bit we received from overseas. We were so thankful to a very special and kind man by the name of Emanual Pflugrath from Ritzville, WA, USA. Mr. Pflugrath had received our name and address through his church. American and Canadian Church organizations were working to help the thousands of displaced people in Europe. After the war had ended, our family was fortunate enough to receive care packages. On one occasion we received a package of coffee. Coffee was a specialty in Germany, not too many people could afford a cup of coffee. We took the coffee and sold it to a dentist in Germany for 360 DM. This money helped us buy bread and potatoes through the black market for our family. Food was very expensive; we were able to buy some food with food ration cards. I was working for a farmer and sometimes was able to buy a bag of potatoes from him. This helped us out quite significantly.

My father started struggling with thoughts as to how he could build a future for our family in Germany. Cities were beginning to be rebuilt. There was so much damage caused from the war. So many homeless people that it was hard visualizing a future for our family. We still were struggling and working hard to go through life. My father and brother Gottlieb were still working at the sawmill as was my second oldest brother Adolf. He was apprenticing in furniture making with very little pay. Unfortunately for me, during my several years of working at the farm, I had hurt my back from heavy lifting. I was admitted to the hospital in Creglingen, and there I had surgery to correct the problem. I was advised by the doctor not to do any hard labor or heavy lifting. After recovery, I started looking for work to help the family. I felt the need to help our family survive.

After the war in 1947, we heard that the USA and Canada were accepting homeless and displaced people. My father began to fill in the immigration forms. It didn't take long before we received a reply from the immigration department, that it was possible to immigrate to Brazil. My father was hesitating to move to Brazil and was requesting immigration forms for Canada. Immigration to Canada was easier if one had sponsors who lived in Canada. The sponsors had to commit themselves to take care of you until you became self-sufficient. With the help of our sponsors we were able to find accommodations and work. These sponsors were responsible for you until citizenship was obtained. My father had a brother living in Canada since 1928. In addition, he had many relatives living in North Dakota, USA.

My father kept busy filing immigration papers. He was leaning toward immigrating to Canada. It was not possible to come up with the money for our whole family of eleven to immigrate to Canada.

In the meantime my father's brother Wilhelm was working to get things started in bringing my family to Canada. With the help from several relatives in Canada, Wilhelm was able to accumulate enough money for 2 people and to have sponsors for them. It was a tough decision as to who was going to immigrate to Canada first. My father decided that at the first opportunity his brothers two children, Amalie and Gottlieb would be the first to be sent. They had no parents and we were not going to leave them behind.

In 1948, we received a message that the fare was

paid and Amalie and Gottlieb were to appear in Breman at the departure station in Germany. Both were required to pass a medical examination. Amalie passed all requirements, but Gottlieb was not as fortunate due to his amputated feet. The condition of Gottlieb was brought forward to his sponsor and more assurances were required from them.

My Uncle Wilhelm in Canada also had a large family and was nearing retirement. Uncertainty was plaguing him with the news of Gottlieb's feet. He was worried that he would have to support Gottlieb if he wasn't able to work. He was not sure that he was able to do so.

Amalie and Gottlieb arrived back in Creglingen. We were waiting for further notification for when Amalie was scheduled to go back to Bremen. Just before Christmas in 1948, word was received for Amalie to go to in Bremen Uberseeheim. Amalie arrived in Bremen, and was loaded on the ship with many more immigrants. She boarded the ship at Christmas time and arrived in Canada on New Year's Day in 1949. My father was glad that her new beginning had started.

We had to be patient for our turn to leave. We were told that immigrating to Brazil was easier. My father said we would wait, and would only go to Brazil if there were no other choices. My father was corresponding with our relatives in the USA. He had made it known to them that we wanted to immigrate to Canada. Some of our relatives pooled together to raise the money for one persons immigration. My father said to me, "Anna you are next in line". I was the oldest of my six siblings.

9
A Fresh Start
(1951-1955)

After I was notified I also had to go by train to Bremen to the Overseas Departure Center. My father again sent my cousin Gottlieb with me. I passed all the medical requirements, but Gottlieb for the second time was declined. We both traveled back to my family in Creglingen and I waited for further notice for my departure. I was not too eager to leave. I did not want to leave my parents and the rest of my family behind. I would imagine myself sailing on the wide-open ocean. I was afraid to go into the unknown venturing to a strange country.

My parents said to me, "Anna this is what we have to do for us to get out of Germany". It was up to me to lead the path to hopefully a better place. I was reassured that the rest of the family would follow me in time. The reason my father pushed so hard for me to apply to go to Canada was that he was so afraid that the Russians would demand that all the people that had fled from the Ukraine to return. It would be horrific to return to Stalin's' dictatorship.

In a short period of time I was notified to arrive at the Overseas Departure Center in Bremen. It was painful to leave for Canada and leave the rest behind. On arrival to Bremen, after a short stay, our ship was ready. I was loaded on the ship toward the end of May 1951. The Swedish ship's name was "MS. ANNA SELEN". After only one day on the ocean I became very seasick. There were more tears shed than one could count. The smell of food turned my stomach. I knew that the food was excellent but I could not eat. Everything was nicely decorated and the staff was all very friendly. When we were approaching the shore of Canada the seasickness had eased off. The "Anna Selen" docked the shore in Canada on June 4, 1951 in Halifax, Nova Scotia where friendly immigration representatives greeted us. We were led to a huge building. All of the immigrants wore their immigration identification tags. We received our train tickets according to the individual destinations. I was given $10.00 cash for food, and then taken to the train station. I was unable to speak the English language; therefore I was too frightened to purchase food. I was frightened and didn't know how to communicate. It was very hard not understanding or speaking the language. Everything was very strange and overwhelming to me. I imagined how things would be when I would reach my destination. At the end of my journey would I be able to recognize my Uncle whom I have never met? There was so much on my mind.

The most frightening experience for me while on the train was when I was ordered out from my sleeping quarter early in the evening. I was led to the back of the train into a caboose. The man that led me was black skinned. I had never seen a dark skinned man before. I was afraid that he was going to harm me. In the caboose was a man doing some paperwork. The dark man brought me a blanket and a pillow. He motioned for me to lie down on a bench. I panicked with fear and shook my head, "No-no-no". I didn't understand that he was trying to help me. The other gentleman, who was working with his papers, must have felt sorry for me and started talking to me, trying to make me understand that I was not in danger. I thought that something bad was going to happen to me, and not being able to tell anyone or escape because of the language barrier. He then started speaking in Ukrainian thinking I may understand. I understood a few words and I could answer some of his questions. Looking back now I understand now what they were doing. I was to change trains in the middle of the night and they kept me separate from the other passengers as not to disturb them. Bringing me a pillow and a blanket was meant for me to rest until I had to change trains.

By the time we reached the destination to where I was to change trains, I was hungry. The train stopped in the province of Saskatchewan. As I was sitting on a bench waiting for the next train, a Chinese Restaurant owner came over to me and motioned with his hands for me to wash dishes. I thought I could do that. There were more people working. After I was finished with the dishes he came and brought me a plate of food. I felt grateful and hungrily started eating. This was my first meal since departure from Halifax, Nova Scotia.

While I was eating, an elderly gentleman came over to my table and started talking German to me. I was so happy that I was able to speak to someone. He told me that his parents immigrated to the USA and then to Canada in the early 1900's. I enjoyed his company and he bought us each a cup of coffee. He stayed and talked with me until I had to board the train. After I was in the train people were staring at me, which made me feel awkward. I had all my identification tags and train tickets pinned on my jacket, these papers were to stay on my jacket until the end of my journey. They were reading where I was destined to go. I felt like I was an outcast. The identification was necessary for the train staff so they were able to make sure I arrived at the right station.

I remember three younger gentlemen boarded the train, wearing huge cowboy hats. I was amazed at their hats. They sat in the seat in front of me. They turned around and noticed my tags and started talking to me in German. They were asking me questions as to where I came from, and I was glad to hear them speaking German. I was happy to learn that some people living in Canada still spoke German. The conductor of the train noticed them talking to me and ordered the boys to turn around and not to talk to me. I was annoyed at the conductor for not allowing them to talk to me. The conductor of the train brought me a book to read. I was confused and upset. Why would the conductor not let us talk together, and instead brought me an English book to read? What was I to do with a book that I could not read? Today I see that what the conductor had done was for my own protection. The staff on the train was responsible for my safe arrival to my destination. I give credit to the immigration department for taking such good care of me.

We traveled through the province of Saskatchewan. Looking out the train window everything was so different to what I was accustomed to. Country homes were planted in the middle of nowhere. I couldn't understand how these people could make a living. I was hoping that I wouldn't have to live this way with nobody around for miles. Could my relatives be living like this too? I had lots of time to ponder in my thoughts as to what kind of life I will have. After a long train ride, which seemed to take forever, I finally heard the train blow its whistle and I saw a small village and the upcoming train station. When the train stopped, I was motioned from the conductor that I was to get off the train. I had arrived at my destination…Leader, Saskatchewan. The letters on my tag, L-E-A-D-E-R, matched the word that was on the sign outside.

As I stepped off the train, I noticed three people standing close by. A man came toward me. He asked in German, "Bischt du Anna"? ("Are you Anna"?) My emotions started flowing and I started crying and said, "yes". He told me that he was my Uncle Wilhelm and he introduced me to my Aunt Christina, my cousin Emanuel, who drove the car. The relatives that I had only seen in pictures were now standing in front of me. We all piled in the vehicle and drove further to a farm in Burstall, Saskatchewan where my Uncle Gottlieb's children were living. There for the first time I was able to meet my Canadian cousins. My Uncle Gottlieb and his wife Katarina had passed away years earlier. Uncle Gottlieb in 1932, and Aunt Katarina in 1939.

I was thinking that how wonderful it would have been if my grandparents were able to have see us all together. After the reunion with my cousins, that evening we drove to my Uncle Wilhelm's farm in the Richmound, Saskatchewan.

The next morning after awakening from my long trip, I looked around at my surroundings and thought how strange everything seemed. My thoughts were with my parents and the rest of my family and how much I missed them. I was worried that the promises my father told me wouldn't come true. I was very homesick for my family and my own familiar surroundings.

After breakfast was finished, I was saying to my

134

Aunt and Uncle that I wanted to work to keep my mind busy. My Uncle meant well and said to me, "Anna take a rest, you are tired after your long journey". The next day I tried to familiarize myself with my surroundings. I walked around the yard, investigated the barn, and inspected the crop that nicely covered the ground. The crop was approximately 4-6 inches tall. It was beautiful, so nice and lush and green, so close to the house. I had never seen this before it was so beautiful.

I stepped out onto the porch and saw several cans on the porch floor. I asked my uncle what they were. He had replied that it was paint for the house. His two sons, Christ and Emanuel were to do the painting. I took it upon myself and started painting the outside walls of the house. In one week the painting was done. There was not much work for me to do on the farm. I could not see myself sitting and doing nothing, this would not bring me an income to help bring my family to Canada. I mentioned to my Uncle Wilhelm that I wished to go to Medicine Hat, Alberta where my two cousins were working. I needed to find work to help my family in Germany. Before I left for Medicine Hat, my Uncle insisted that we drive to Richmound, Saskatchewan where we stopped at the general store. He wanted to buy something for me in appreciation for the work I had done. I saw in the first few days the living conditions my Uncle's family was living under. They had their clothing and shelter, which was the most important thing in life, but not much extra to speak of. I knew they were struggling and didn't have the money. Living in the country you had your meat, eggs and flour. My Uncle insisted, and I chose a plastic apron for the cost of $0.25.

The next day my cousin Emanuel drove me to Medicine Hat, Alberta. My two cousins both had jobs in the city. My cousin Amalie was working in a restaurant, and Kay was working at the Dominion Glass Factory. Through Amalie I got a job working at the Savoy Café where I washed dishes. I was glad to have a job. There were not too many options for work due to the language barrier besides restaurant or greenhouse work. My $0.25 apron came in very handy at the restaurant.

My job demanded long hours of shift work and very low wages. I managed to save every penny, not even allowing myself to spend a penny on myself. I was saving up to bring my family to Canada. I am very thankful to my cousin Kaye. She had paid the extra rent for me for three months while staying in her basement suite she rented. It was a one- bedroom basement suite. I never thought for a moment to ask her what I owed for rent. I was very young and naïve. Kaye made better money at the Glass Factory where she worked. She also helped her family out financially who lived in Medicine Hat. I was able to save my small salary for when it came time to bring my parents and siblings over to Canada.

Back in Germany my father was working diligently on the immigration papers for Canada. And on the Canadian end of things, our relatives were helping in every way possible. I had saved $170.00 in the short time I was working in Canada. There were still eight family members as well as my cousin Gottlieb in Germany. It was going to be hard to bear the cost of bringing my entire family to Canada.

Before bringing my entire family to Canada, my

Uncle Wilhelm and my cousin Ben Roth had signed papers that they had sufficient accommodations for our whole family. They were also responsible to support the family till we found jobs and to be able to support ourselves. My father told his brother in Canada that they would not have to worry, we will be on our own soon, and we had five persons in the family capable of working. We worked all our lives, my family was not afraid of hard work.

Before my family started proceedings to immigrate to Canada, my father made arrangements with Ida Hoffman, the lady who had brought our cousin Gottlieb out of the Russian zone that Gottlieb could stay with their family until we had arrangements made in Canada to bring Gottlieb out of Germany.

My father applied through the Lutheran Mission in Canada, which to my understanding worked together with the Lutheran mission in Germany. The churches helped to pay for the German displaced people to immigrate to the US and Canada. Our family was very fortunate to receive this help from the Lutheran Mission in Winnipeg, Manitoba. Since I was already in Canada, it was more readily possible to get the help we needed. With the monies combined from relatives and what I had saved, the Lutheran Mission would make up the shortfall. Now it was possible for my entire family to immigrate to Canada.

I was so happy that our goals had been reached and our wishes fulfilled. Soon my family would be all together in Canada, in the Land of the Free! I started to look for housing accommodations for my family to live in. I was lucky to find a small basement suite in the Flats area on 12th St. SE for rent with two small bedrooms and a tiny kitchen.

October 12, 1951 my whole family arrived in Canada. Unfortunately my cousin Gottlieb Roth had once again been denied access.

Our family was welcomed with open arms from our relatives. A welcome party was held for us. My parents were helped out with the necessities of life. Our relatives supplied flour, potatoes, and vegetables. Not knowing a word of English, finding work for all would be a difficult task. We soon found that the people in Medicine Hat were helpful and kind. Medicine Hat was home for many German people. We were introduced to the Evangelical Church, and there it was made known that my father and my two brothers were looking for work. Every Sunday we went to church. We welcomed the opportunity to become friends in our new land. It didn't take us younger folk long to find our way around Medicine Hat. Medicine Hat in the 1950's was not very big. The transition was a little more difficult for my mother as she didn't get out of her little environment within the house. I felt sorry for her, having no education she missed out on a lot. One incident in particular on a Sunday morning; she wasn't feeling well to go to church so she stayed home while the rest of us went on our way. After my mother finished her cup of coffee, she turned the radio on, and heard the most beautiful German songs sung on the program "The Lutheran Hour" broadcast from Winnipeg, Manitoba. She was so homesick when she heard the singing and she wanted to save the songs by turning the radio off until my father came home from church thinking that they would be able to listen to the music together. As soon as my father, Karl came through the door switching the radio on, she said, "Karl, listen to the nice German songs on the radio." To her dismay, the German songs were no longer there; she thought the radio worked like a record player. My father had to explain to her how a radio worked, that the songs don't stay. We all had a good chuckle, but mother felt hurt and embarrassed.

My younger siblings went to school, and my mother was home alone all day long. She passed her days with cooking, baking, laundry and cleaning. There were many times that one could tell that tears had swelled in her eyes for she was so homesick and lonely. Had that ocean not have separated the two countries, we were sure she would have returned to Germany if she had the money and family on her side.

We often found mother looking through papers upside down in her hands. My mother would hold the hymnal book in church upside down and sing, trying not to let on to the people surrounding her that she could not read. To my surprise, my mother knew so many songs by heart. My father and mother would sit in their veranda on Sunday's after dinner and sing. They harmonized very well together, I was proud of how my mother taught herself, she was a person that never gave up, she was determined. It was sad that my mother was not able to attend school. Her adopted parents had never sent her to school. They used her to do the hard work. At the age of eight years she had to milk cows and kneed bread dough. She never was able to sign her own name. When she needed to sign a document, she marked it with an "X". She asked to learn how to write her name. She was so proud when she mastered "O R-O-T-H". This was the only thing she was able to write.

Rev. Vorrath acquainted himself with us from the

church; he was very kind and took the time and took my father to find work. My father found work in a Brick and Tile Factory in Redcliff, Alberta. Redcliff was approximately seven km from Medicine Hat. My brothers Gottlieb and Adolf found work with farmers over the winter months. They earned $25.00 per month. We were glad we all had work, and a roof over our heads. My sister Hilda, at the age of 14 was also helping out on the farm at relatives.

After one year in Canada, my cousin Gottlieb was still in Germany. More assurance was needed from our family and relatives for Gottlieb to immigrate to Canada. Finally, in 1952, Gottlieb was able to immigrate to Canada. Our family now was truly complete.

We continued our daily routines, and we were all happy. In the spring of 1952, Medicine Hat was hit with a flood and our little basement suite also took the wrath. We lost the little bit we had. We walked away with the clothes on our backs. We once again looked for shelter. We found shelter with relatives for a short while, and later found a small basement suite on Dominion St. SE. We were happy we found a new place to stay.

My father worked very hard, loading bricks onto train cars. He was completely exhausted by the time he came home in the evenings. Many times he would tell us that the freedom that we now have is worth the hard work. We prayed that we would maintain our health, which is most important in life. Father was working very hard, sometimes to the breaking point. We saw how the hard work almost took the life out of him. But our father didn't give up. Looking back for his age he worked way

too hard.   At the Brick & Tile he had to load the train
boxcars with tile, which you had to lift by hand. When he
came home from work, all he had energy for was to eat
and then he rested for the next day's work. The job was
hard physically, but he stuck to it.

My cousin Ben Roth was working at a construction
company. It was through Ben that my brother Adolf
acquired a job working at "Johnson Construction". Adolf
was familiar in the construction business since he was
apprenticing in Germany to build furniture. My other
brother Gottlieb began working with my father at the Brick
& Tile. I began my second job working in a greenhouse,
"Robb's Greenhouse". We were always on the lookout for
better paying jobs.

My sister Hilda came to Medicine Hat after helping
on the farm. I found work for Hilda at the same
greenhouse that I worked at.

Looking back, for us young immigrants we lived a
very dull and lonesome life. Sunday mornings were a great
time for us as this was our only social time. Sundays was
our day to build up energy for the next weeks work and to
go to church. As a family we all worked together. Each
payday, all our earnings were handed over to our parents.
My father opened a bank account at "The Bank of
Montreal" in which all cheques were deposited. Only
enough was held back for living expenses. My family's goal
was to purchase our own home. We wanted to have a
house to call our own.

In 1953 we were able to purchase our own small
home for the price of $8000.00. This was a large amount of

money in that era. My parents were full of excitement. My father made a down payment to Mr. Wilhelm Meier, the former owner of the house. The house purchased was on 5th Street SE in the flats area. Agreement for sale of purchase was $200.00 per month. This house still stands to this day.

I could see the happiness in our family, especially my parents. They were now owners of their own little house, our home. We all were working now to pay off our debts. We had paid back the Lutheran Mission and now had payments to make for the house. Without the five people working and bringing home their paychecks, this wouldn't have been possible.

We had our freedom and the gratitude of having the necessities of life…. food, clothing, and shelter.
Our family was thankful to God that we no longer had the suffering we had to endure in the past. Our ancestors sacrificed so much for us to have a better life and future.

There were still times I felt guilt, grief and sorrow as we now had so much and the ones that fell in the hands of the Polish and the Russians after WW11. Most of our relatives were deported to Siberia, Kazakhstan and Arhangelsk. They had to endure so much misery in their life. They were thousands of miles away but dear in our hearts. From 1927 – 1953 during Stalin's rule, Stalin was responsible for eliminating millions of people by forcing them to work in hard labor camps. His foresight was to build up the Soviet Union and was determined to obtain World Power with the cost of human lives.

Many times I felt guilt ridden that now in Canada we had freedom and plenty to eat and our relatives in Siberia were starving. My thoughts were with my Aunts, Uncles and cousins with whom I have grown up. The hardest was not having any sort of communication with them. Right after the German war, people were still considered spies and traitors against Russia. They were terribly mistreated and living in terrible conditions. In my heart I didn't lose hope that someday we would hear from our people.

As time passed by, slowly some occasional news reached us through the Red Cross. In 1955 German Counselor, Dr. Adenauer was allowed to pay a visit to Russia and to meet the Russian leader Nikita Kruschov and to discuss the Germans that were held in captivity under the "Komendatur". In the same year they were to be given more freedom to travel in and around the surrounding areas. A document was to be signed that they would not be allowed to go back to their birthplaces of the Volga region, Ukraine and Odessa. Slowly the Russian-Germans were given permission to settle in Asia. It took several years till this came into affect and they were still detained by the Russian government, as the low-paying manpower was needed in Siberia to build canals, bridges, railroad track and more. The German-Russia people put their trust in Dr. Adenaur's hands and were waiting patiently to be able to go home to their ancestors land, Germany. The German Germans (individuals born with German citizenships) were the first ones to be freed back to Germany. Russia did not acknowledge the German-Russian people to return to Germany and were held back. With more decisions and meetings with the Russian Leader, Kruschov and the German Counselor Dr. Adenouer the Germans from

Russia were allowed to a little more freedom. After many years in captivity, slowly the Germans from Russia were allowed into Germany. We were happy to receive the news that my cousin Amalia Korp (nee Schorzmann) and Waldemar Zimmerman with family from Kazakhstan in Siberia had made it safely to Germany out of Russia. I was hoping and praying that someday we will have the opportunity to reunite again. It was worth all the tears and worries to know that some of our loved ones survived and it was God's blessing.

As long as I was still at home and single, I always worked very hard. Being the oldest of my siblings, I felt I carried more responsibility, and more worries. My biggest aim was to see that my parents were taken care of. I never did shy away from work. I found the language barrier difficult, but I was always striving for jobs with better pay. I worked two jobs; one at the restaurant, and the second job was working at Robb's Greenhouse. It was fine; it suited me as most of the workers spoke German. Even the owner was German. But the pay didn't satisfy me. My cousin Kaye Roth was working at Dominion Glass Factory, and told me that they were hiring. I wasn't afraid of the work. I was afraid of not being able to understand English, nor was I able to properly reply back. One day I decided to take the chance and I applied for the job at the Factory. To my surprise I was hired, and I was to be at the job by midnight for my first shift. I worked from midnight to 8 o'clock in the morning. Now my real worries started, I was pinned between two jobs. I didn't have time to give the job at the greenhouse notice of quitting. I was not so sure if the job at the factory would be permanent. I was very afraid that I would not be in a position to stay at that job only because my English was very poor. I thought about what kind of the mess I got myself into. It came close to the time where I had to take the bus to Redcliff, which was seven miles from Medicine Hat. When I arrived at the factory there was not much time, I just went and copied what the other workers were doing. I was advised what my job would entail. I was stationed where I would unfold and stencil carton boxes. Now I knew my job, to unfold and mark the boxes. I was hoping that neither the boss nor foreman would come by and ask me a question. What would happen if I didn't understand? All worries aside the first night went by smoothly. I was hoping it would go that smooth for the whole shift, which was seven days. It was fast and repetitious work. I was not afraid. I knew I would be able to keep up. At shift change, 8:00 in the morning, we would punch our time cards and went straight into the bus that was waiting outside to transport us back to Medicine Hat. Most factory workers were from the Medicine Hat area. When the bus reached its stop, I literally ran all the way home, which took approximately 10 minutes. I would run into the house, change clothing, and off to work at the greenhouse. One time I was one hour late when my mother was in the hospital. I used the excuse that I had to get my younger siblings off to school. To make up for that hour I had to work through my lunch hour. This excuse worked for a few days then my boss started to getting a little suspicious. It was now time to come clean and tell the truth about having two jobs. I myself felt guilty, so I quit at the greenhouse with apologies to the boss. By now I felt exhausted. After my mother was released from the hospital she had found out I working two jobs. She said to me, "how long you think you can go on like this, working almost steady?" After quitting at the greenhouse I felt more at ease that I only had to focus on my one job at the factory. As long as we were living under my parents' roof, we felt obligated to help with paying the bills. Every payday we would hand our paycheck to my mother. Mother would deposit it in the bank, In the event that I needed to purchase something, I would ask my mother for money, but it had better be a good reason. We ate good home cooked meals and had clothes on our backs; no more suffering. While we were living in our new adopted homeland, we called it "The Land of the Free".

I worked myself up in the factory, and found some of the girls were very helpful. Maybe they felt sympathetic towards me because of my poor English. Sometimes the foreman would walk by and ask questions and I didn't understand what he was saying. One day he came from the office with a book and asked me a question. I could not respond, I didn't understand what he was saying. The girl on the assembly line came quickly asking, "Was ish die punch numre?" I was surprised that she could speak a little German and I told her what my punch number was. Before and after work you had to punch your time card so it registered the starting time and quitting time at work. The girl's name that helped me was Ann Mastel.

I started at the factory in the middle of 1952 and worked full time until Christmas break. I received notice, along with other workers that we would be laid off until further notice. I was a little scared. Rumors were going around that it could be a long layoff. There was nothing anybody could do. I was hoping that after the Christmas season I would be able to start up again. I was living at home with my family, but I felt sorry for some of the girls that came and were living in Medicine Hat and had to pay rent and live from paycheck to paycheck. I couldn't understand why they weren't able to save a little money.

146

Well I guess we were brought up different. I had gone through a much tougher life. Before we were laid off we all received a little Xmas gift and a box of Christmas glassware. We were told that they would call if someone called in sick. They didn't say whom they would call, but it would be random. After I was laid off, I didn't leave the house, in hopes that I would receive a call to go in to work. Sure enough, the phone rang. I lifted the phone, and on the other end I heard, "Miss Roth, could you come in for work?" It was early enough in the day for me to still catch the bus. I was so glad I was back at work after New Year's. I wasn't sure whether it was going to be permanent or if I was filling in for somebody who was sick. But at least it was another day's work for pay. I felt lucky, as I was called out more and more. The young girls wanted to go to parties on the weekends and would phone in at the last minute, so I received another call, but it was too late to catch the bus. I was brought into work by taxi by the factory. I got to think that if they go that far to pay a taxi for me to come to work, they must feel that I am dependable, and must like the job I was doing.

Not long after the holidays, and everything went back to a normal routine, I was once again back at work full time. I think my family was happy to be able to use the phone, as I had been literally beside the phone so I would not miss the call. If any of my family members used the phone, they always had to tell their friends that they were not allowed to use the phone too long as we were waiting for a phone call. Many times my siblings teased me for sitting for hours beside the phone. When I went back to work I was transferred from stenciling boxes to sorting glassware. There were three people to sort and pack the glassware. They manufactured different types of glasses,

147

canning jars, wine and pop bottles, ashtrays, and many other glassware. When you entered the work area a person was able to look at a sheet on the wall and there you would find which area you were to work in and that was your job for the day. Everyday you would have to check to where and what job you would be doing. The work was fast and steady, and I worked hard, and I worked myself up to $1.45/hr.which was good money back in the 1950's. Our past experiences made us grow up fast. We were needed to help support the family; we never were able to take part in teenage functions such as parties or dances. We felt that going to parties was a waste of time and money, as this was the first time in our lives to make something out of ourselves. Plus, our father forbade us. Working full time at the glass factory, I was entitled to one-week holiday. Now my parents owned the little house and I was living with our big family. My cousin, Martha Bechthold (nee Roth) and her husband Henry were farming approximately 60 miles northeast of Medicine Hat. Every time they came to the city they would drop in to visit us. It just happened that I had just started my holiday. Martha asked me if I would like to come out to their farm. She asked if I would help her in her house on the farm. I didn't want to refuse so I agreed to go along with them.

It was much more peaceful out in the country. There was always somebody dropping in at my cousins. One of the neighbors from the surrounding area stopped in, I didn't know the people so I kept doing other things. I always found something to do. During my stay I helped butcher a few chickens for Sunday dinner. I loved the fresh chicken and gravy. After the weekend it was time for Martha and Henry to take me back to Medicine Hat. I needed a little time to prepare to start my job in the factory.

148

Cousin Martha with her family paid a short visit with my parents, and then they left to do some errands, and some grocery shopping before heading back to the country. My cousin Martha was telling me later that a young farmer from the same area came by for some farm business. Martha said to the young farmer, calling him by name and said, "Fred you should have dropped in last week, we had company from the Hat". I think she would make a good farmer's wife she doesn't shy away from work. She is my cousin Anna. On my next day off Martha had planned to stop in for a visit and I had my hair in curlers. I had heard Martha's voice and went into the living room, and said, "Oh you are in town again". Martha replied, "Jah, we had things to do and we brought a neighbor along". Martha introduced her neighbor to me as Fred Fischer. After visiting for a while Martha said, "How about we all go to a movie"? After the movie, they dropped me off at home, and I got out of the vehicle. Fred had than asked me when I had my next day off again and I told him when that was. Not thinking anything of it, I went inside and went to bed. It was a little after nine in the evening and the younger ones were still up. The next day I started work at my old routine for the week. As my workweek neared and the day came to have off, I was looking forward to staying home and resting up for the next stretch of working days. Again, on my days off work as I was looking out the window I saw a truck parked out front of our house. I noticed it was the same guy I met through my cousin. I went to the door, I said, "Oh you're in town again" with a sheepish grin. He replied, "Yes", He had business to do in town. He asked if I would like to go to a movie again. I thought quickly and said "OK". After Fred brought me home, Fred asked if I would mind if he came in on my next day off. He seemed to be a nice guy and I said if you have the time, I would like if you would come in. He told me that he lived with his mother on the farm and it was in spring, which meant he was busy with his cattle. He said that his cows would be calving soon. From then on, Fred came to Medicine Hat every time on my days off. Fred got acquainted with my parents. My father liked Fred. They always had nice visits and lots to talk about. Fred became a regular visitor. Sometimes he stayed for a meal, or sometimes just for a coffee. My mother baked Schlitz keechlla often. It seemed Fred liked my family. He was saying that his mother made them too, but they weren't as fancy. Now it looked as though Fred was my farmer boyfriend. Every time Fred came, my siblings would say, "Anna, your boyfriend is here". One Saturday night, Fred brought his mother with him. Mrs. Fischer wanted to visit her sister, and it just so happened that her sister was not home, so Fred brought Mrs. Fischer to our house. We invited them in, my father was a very talkative man, and knew from Fred that his parents had emigrated in the earlier years from the Ukraine. My parents had struck an interesting conversation about the past and the old country. Mrs. Fischer was telling my dad that they had come from Alexanderfeld in the Ukraine. Fred would come in quite regularly, and my family didn't mind. Fred was liked and respected by my family. Sometimes Fred couldn't make it into town and my family would ask, "Isn't Fred coming in today?", as though they were missing him. The next time I saw Fred I had asked him if his mother had enjoyed her visit with us. Fred had said that she enjoyed the visit, and then silence fell. I had the feeling Fred was holding something back. Not saying anything Fred said, "Anna, I will tell you what my mother said on the way home. She had absolutely nothing good to say about you. She had asked, "What do you want with her?" She saw so many faults in you. It made Fred very

angry, and he said that she never even knew you. I told
Fred that he has to try to forgive her because she is still his
mother. Fred had said this was not the first time that she
had said things about others. I had asked Fred that could it
not be that one-day you would find someone and she
would be afraid of losing you? Fred replied, "I had never
thought of it that way, but maybe you hit the nail on the
head". I said, "Don't ever forget that she is still your
mother". Fred said that maybe he shouldn't have said
anything. From my point of view, I said, "I think you did
the right thing, you are an honest man". Fred asked, "now
that I told you can I still come to see you?" I told Fred that
he had become the best friend that I ever had, and he gave
me a big hug. He seemed to be happier and spoke more
freely. The day went by fast and was now past my bedtime.
It was time for Fred to leave for the farm. After two weeks
Fred came to Medicine Hat and offered me a ride to the
country to see his farm. He wanted to show what he was
doing and show me where he lived. He also had a surprise
for me. When we got out to the farm, he had hired a bunch
of natives (but in those days Canadians referred to them as
Indians) to pick rocks off of the new land breaking. I could
not believe my eyes. There were huge rocks lying all over
the field. From a distance Fred pointed out the homestead.
Fred said that if his mother (old lady) wasn't home, he
would take me to see the house, but we were sure Mrs.
Fischer saw us driving around. I had told Fred that it would
be better to drop in and say hi. So we proceeded on to the
farmyard. The house was built in 1929 and was one of the
better houses for that time; it just needed some paint.
When we entered the farmhouse I knew Mrs. Fischer had
seen us driving around, she was not at all surprised to see
me. Mrs. Fischer was trying hard to be friendly, but I could
sense that she truly didn't care too much for me. I was

sitting alone with her in the kitchen; I didn't know what to say to her. I was sure glad when a neighbor's vehicle came into the yard. I felt relief that someone else was present, but I was not introduced to her visitor. Mrs. Fischer was talking to her visitor and I just minded my own business. After a few minutes Fred came and was ready to take me back to Medicine Hat. Fred was telling me that the visitor was Matilda Schafer. Then Fred made a remark, "those two fit together, now they can talk all they want." I never did ask questions about this remark. I changed the subject by admiring the green fields and the lush hills on the way into Medicine Hat. With Fred driving back and forth, a lot of time for him was lost where he had so much work to do. His cattle were calving; he needed to be home to tend to them. So by the end of July, Fred proposed to me. I was surprised, so soon after we had met. We had only dated a short time. He had said that when he met my family he considered them to be a nice respectful family, and that I was a nice girl. I didn't give him an answer right away. I told my parents the Fred had proposed, asking for their advice. They told me to do what I thought was right. Now I was struggling between getting married or staying at home and keeping my factory job. It was not easy making a choice between losing my income and getting married.

My Uncle Wilhelm Roth came to Medicine Hat from the farm in Richmound, and my parents mentioned about the marriage proposal to my uncle. As I came into the door, my Uncle Wilhelm said that he has been hearing news that I was going to be a farmer's wife. I replied, "Oh, Uncle Whilhelm, I'm not sure yet." Uncle Wilhelm said that he knew the Fischer family and they were good people, and I couldn't go wrong. I think you would make a good farmer's wife. Uncle Wilhelm was saying to me, "I would take the chance, you are 27 years old, and it's time to leave the nest." Even with all of Uncle Wilhelm's encouragement, I was still apprehensive. For the first time in my life, I was earning money. Fred wasn't able to come in, and I was somewhat relieved, it bought me time to think things through. The things that Uncle Wilhelm had said kept going through my mind, I was 27 years old, should I take the chance, or stay single and work in the factory. In those days I was classified as an old maid. The following week, Fred came into town, it had been my turn to clean the house that day, and Fred had asked me if I had time to think about what he had asked me two weeks prior being quite persistent that he needed to know before he went downtown. I knew what Fred was up to. He had wanted to see if I was going to accept his proposal, and then he was going to buy a suit. I told him that the decision was hard for me to make. I told him that I would marry him, as he was a nice fellow. Fred felt so relieved and happy. We drove downtown and parked his truck and started walking down the streets of downtown. We walked to a men's clothing store, where Fred started trying on suits. Once Fred found the one he liked, he purchased it for $140.00. After he bought the suit we went to the jewelry store where we looked at rings. Fred asked me to pick out a wedding ring set. I made sure as to pick a more reasonable priced set as we always were told by our parents not to buy the most expensive things. The jeweler took out the rings and Fred told me to put the engagement ring on. As we left the store Fred piped up and said, "now we're engaged." Fred then took me home to finish my house cleaning.

Week after week went by, and Fred continued to come to Medicine Hat to see me. One weekend Fred had come in and said, "It is very hard for me to come in every weekend, there is so much work to do on the farm." He had said that we should get married soon. The only thing we needed to do was to find a small house for his mother to live in. She didn't want to leave the farm. I said that it would be ok for her to stay, as the house was big enough. I would have more time to help in the fields and his mother would be able to stay in the house and deal with the house chores. Fred replied, "It would never work, I know my mother, she will move close to her sister, so she won't be lonesome." I said to Fred, "Won't it be hard on your mother?" Fred replied, "Yes it will, but you don't know my mother, you've never had the chance to really get to know her." Fred implied that his mother was somewhat of a gossip in the community.

It was now July, and harvest was just around the corner. It was now time to give my notice to quit at work. My boss was not very happy. Meanwhile Fred was making all the arrangements for our wedding. The hall was booked, and the date set for August 12, 1955, which just so happened to be my birthday. We were married in the Evangelical Lutheran Church in Medicine Hat officiated by Pastor Riegal. The next day after our wedding, we started moving out to the farm to start my new life. Fred's family and the neighbors in the surrounding area all spoke German so there was no language barrier to cross. This made me feel quite at home.

10
Farm Life
(1955-1969)

We made our home on the Fischer homestead. Life on the farm was hard work. Farm life was a new fresh start for me. Some crop years were not so good, wheat prices were low, but that was farm life. Fred often said that farming is a gamble. We didn't have much money, but neither did anyone else in the community. Everyone had the same struggles. But we were happy. We never went hungry. Fred was a very handy man, you name it, he could fix it, and he was a jack-of-all-trades. Fred never gave up until his work was done, whether it was welding, electrical work, mechanics, he even had a knack for veterinary work. When trouble arose the surrounding area farmers called upon Fred for his vet skills. He was happy to help out.

We both would try to stretch the few dollars that we had. Only the necessities were purchased such as spices, sugar, rice and cleaning supplies. We raised our own livestock so we had our own milk, cheese, eggs and meat. From our grain we had our own flour. I would bake up to 6-8 loaves of bread weekly. Fred loved the German made dough dishes. He was raised on the same German foods as I was.

In January 1, 1957 our first son, Bruce Fischer, was born. Fred was proud to become a father, and he visualized that a new little farmer had been born. On November 26, 1958 our second son was born, his name was Dale Wesley. It was hard having two babies to take care of as well as all the outside chores. October 9, 1959 our twin girls, Audrey

Marie and Melinda Ann were born. Taking care of the children was an all around the clock work. After all the babies were in bed, I started working through the night washing diapers. We had no hot running water so I had to heat the water on the wood stove first. I had no dryer, and diapers were hanging all over the house. There was no money for new clothes so mending was endless. When I think back there was no time for myself. It seemed I never got rest. It is truly amazing what one can endure when you must. Where there is a will, there is a way. My whole life I worked firstly for my parents and siblings and now worked for my own husband and our children. It was hard to succeed and make a living off the land, the wheat prices were low, and by the time the bills were paid, there was not much left.

I especially loved living on the farm. I loved my life and the freedom. I regret not being able to share my dark past with Fred. He did not live under those conditions that I had to live and grow up with, and he didn't understand what I went through. He was born in a free country, and couldn't understand what it was like living under the communist regime. I had a feeling that I was never fully taken seriously, so I kept a lot of those feelings inside. Deep inside in my heart I was mourning and crying in silence. I remember so many times preparing a nice fresh chicken dinner, I thought about my loved ones in Siberia. We have an abundance of food and my own people were starving. I asked God how he could let this happen. I needed to move on and focus on my family.

My brother Adolf and his family often came to the farm on weekends for a visit. The trip was only 65 miles from Medicine Hat, AB. I was always happy to see them. It was not very often we drove to Medicine Hat. Only for Doctor appointments or other important appointments. Adolf was now a professional carpenter building houses. Fred and Adolf would build granaries on the farm and also built our little butcher house. Adolf built my first cupboards in the kitchen. I was so proud to have such a novelty. My sister-in-law Margaret helped me out with my chores. Margaret loved helping herself to our thick heavy cream and fresh butter.

My brother's children and my children would play freely on the farm. It made me happy when Fred and my children were happy. The children went to the four-room country school in Horsham, Saskatchewan. The children were bused to school every day, and arrived home each day happy to see their father work in his shop and to go on with their adventures and chores. Dale was especially fond of his cats. Every one of my children had their own interests. Audrey and Melinda were always fascinated with sewing. At five years old they would sit at the sewing machine making clothes for the dolls. Bruce was always daddy's boy. Dale was the artist in the family. No matter where their interests lie, we loved them all dearly.

On November 22, 1969 Fred passed away suddenly leaving me alone with four children. Everything was taken from us. Our lives were shattered. I cannot express on paper the emptiness my children and myself went through. The decision was made that it would be best that the children and I move to Medicine Hat. It was winter and it worried me if one of the children would get sick, we had no phone in the house and I couldn't drive. The country roads were not in the best of shape for traveling in the winter months. I wasn't able to think straight. I was in shock. I

157

was afraid of being alone. My parents stayed with me and the children on the farm for two weeks until the children's Christmas break from school. It was sad and lonesome without Fred. I wasn't able to drive, so with the help of family and relatives we moved to Medicine Hat with my parents. Since Fred had no will made, all assets were frozen. I was forced to auction off the livestock and machinery. I kept the farmland and rented it out. The four children and I stayed at my parents small home for eight months. After Fred's estate was finally settled, my brother Adolf built us our new home in Medicine Hat. In July of 1970 we were able to move into our own home. I went to look for work to support the family. I was now father and mother to them. As I had knowledge in sewing, I started working in a drapery shop. I had befriended my co-worker Ruby Crockford and together in 1972 we opened our own drapery business, "Ru-Ann Draperies. In 1976 I bought my partner out and "Fischer's Draperies" was born. The drapery business became a thriving family business.

In the early 1970's, the Good Samaritan, Mr. Emanuel Pflugrath, who had shipped packages to us in Germany, had the opportunity to visit with my parents in Medicine Hat, AB, Canada. It was an honor for my parents to meet this kind person. My parents were so happy to have been able to travel to the USA and meet relatives that they had never met before. He was able to relate with these people, they shared many of their memories together. From the Hebron, ND Parish he met Rev. John G. Lind, Gidian Ketterling, (ND), Christian Roth (Elgen, ND), Matheis Schimpp (Elgen, ND), Pastor R. Kirschenmann (Ritzville, WA).

The drapery business was now operating for 10 years

and quite successful. I had saved up enough money for my daughter Melinda and I to go to Germany to visit with relatives that I hadn't seen for 38 years. We were booked to visit Germany for three weeks. I am so happy to have been able to visit my cousins Amalie Korp and Waldemar Zimmerman. Amalie and I had so much to talk about, the past and the present. We knew each other in the early days as school friends, and we shared all the terrible things we went through. In those days we never ventured past our surroundings, and all the surrounding kids were friends. Amalie told me that looking back, it was a miracle that we survived what we went through. We reminisced how my Aunt Otilia would try and teach us how to embroider. We would always try to out do one another!

Amalie shared one of her experiences during the war with me. This is what she shared with me:

While still under Russian rule living in the barracks in Poland they were packed into railway boxcars traveling deep into the wilderness of Siberia. In the barracks there, one could see through the cracks of the walls. The winds would come whistling through and made the barracks icy cold. They were forced to walk in the forest, sometimes 3 km to fell trees. The snow was deep and the temperature extremely cold. They didn't have the proper clothing for the climate. There were so many sick people and were lice infested. She would tell me that when she took her stockings off, you could literally see the stocking move from the lice. Walking in the forest, every hump that one encountered, was more than likely a dead body. It was in Siberia they saw the many barracks filled with prisoners. The German prisoners were regarded as traitors against the Soviet Union and the Stalin's regime. They saw the suffering in the eyes among the prisoners. They saw what their futures held. The life these people went through was indescribable. They knew there was no help or changes to come; they would all die out in the wilderness. The little bit of energy left in their bodies was going to be drained with the hard labour, which lay ahead. The cost of human life was atrocious, and many young girls were beaten and raped by the Russian security. They were stripped of any dignity they had left.

Amalie and I sat there crying having no control over our emotions. A few days went by and Amalie and I made plans to visit our cousin Waldemar Zimmerman. We drove toward Frankfurt where Waldemar lived. On arrival at Waldemar's house, we found him in his garden, where he was tending to his birds. It was a relaxing environment to be in. Waldemar was not able to work, as he was almost blind. We were very happy to see each other after so many years. We had so much to talk about. Waldemar never stopped talking, his words were bubbling out of his mouth. He spoke of our young years in the Ukraine. In his young years, Waldemar's parents were separated and he stayed with his mother. His father still helped the family by giving the odd loaf of bread. They lived very poorly, as did everyone else at that time. Waldemar said, "Anna, remember how we kids had to steal for our survival, we stole just to feed ourselves." With a slight smirk on his face, Waldemar reminisced about the time he and his friends were hungry, and went out to look for food. They walked for hours, and nothing was to be found. They were very thirsty and no wells around in the area. On the other side of Johannestal, in an easterly direction, were a strip of bushes and trees. They noticed that the cows from the collective were returning to the dams for water. As the cows came closer to the dam the cows started running towards the water. It was a very hot day. Waldemar and his two friends were also running along side the herd. As the cattle settled down Waldemar and his two friends, were so hungry and thirsty, and they decided to go milk a cow. They each started milking a cow and squirted the milk into their mouths until they were full. They then headed back toward their homes, feeling quite good about themselves. Waldemar said that looking back it sounds hilarious, but one does what needs to be done when hungry.

Waldemar went on to talk about having to flee from their home, and I realized they went through the same experience as my family and I went through. Every one of us had a different experience, some worse than others. Waldemar was telling us that after the Russian Army occupied Poland, the German people were herded worse than cattle into barracks, and then they were loaded into closed wagons, packed like sardines in a can. There was very little room to turn. Women and children were crying. Day after day the train kept pushing deeper North into the coldest part of Siberia with only short stops, out in the middle of nowhere. Sometimes a few loaves of dry, heavy bread were thrown into the boxcars to divide among the people. Waldemar said that he was reloaded and sent off to Karaganda, northern direction of Kazakhstan. Waldemar was only 15 years old at the time. He was telling me the same story of how the barracks were so cold, no warm clothing and food was scarce. They were not allowed to cut a tree for warming up the barracks. They were only allowed to pick small sticks off the ground to burn for heat. Waldemar was ordered to work at the coal mine. The hours were long, and every day a quota was to be filled, and if that certain amount was not filled, food was not provided.

He worked many months of hard labor until an explosion occurred. Waldemar was hurt in the coalmine from that explosion.

Efforts were made to rescue hurt people within the coal mine. The people who showed signs of life were taken to the hospital for treatment. The ones that showed no sign of life were taken to a building and covered with sheets. Waldemar told us he was among the ones listed as dead. Three days after the explosion, laborers came to dispose of the dead bodies. Bodies were taken out of the building, and when they picked him up, they discovered that Waldemar was still alive, and partially conscious. He couldn't move or see, and totally blind. He was rushed to the hospital and the doctors tried skin grafts on his whole body. His body was full of small pieces of coal imbedded in his skin even in his eyes and the doctors were not able to help him. His best friend and guide was a Seeing Eye Dog. He was so frustrated and even suicidal at times. He thought that he would have been better off dead, but then he thought that he was still too young to die. As the years passed, seeing his doctors, he began to see flickers of daylight. He was filled with new hope and excitement. His doctor had to report to the authorities that Waldemar might improve. As his eyesight was slightly improving, his government assistance was cut short. He still had in mind that he wanted to leave Russia. Eventually he did immigrate to Germany and he was still thankful for the few years in his life to be able to live a peaceful life in Germany. In 1985, Waldemar passed away in Germany.

In 1996 we received word that two more of our relatives arrived in Germany from Siberia and Asia, my cousins, Rosa Diede and Amalie Marchel. The news was overwhelming. I got in touch with them; I was apprehensive to travel to Germany alone so I had asked my brother Adolf and his wife Margret to accompany me. Arrangements were made and we departed on a plane to Germany.   It was wonderful to be reunited with the cousins with whom I played with every day in my younger years. I was wondering throughout the whole flight if I would be able to recognize my cousin or they me. I made a sign, which said "Happy Reunion after 52 years" so they would be able to spot us. We arrived at the Frankfurt airport. I was holding my sign for my cousins to identify me. After meeting my cousins, after more than 50 years o f separation, we felt more like strangers meeting for the first time, as the last time we saw each other we were children. It was difficult to grasp what had happened in each of our lives.

Rosa started to reveal her terrible experience to us. We were separated from the camps in Poland. We talked endlessly. Many tears were shed between us, sometimes crying uncontrollable while Rosa was telling me of her experiences in Siberia. Sometimes Rosa became so emotional that she could not continue with revealing her past. It was very hard to relive these times. In 1947 her mother and father died very close together of starvation in Siberia. With the help from others she buried her own parents beside a large tree in unmarked graves. Standing in the wilderness in front of her parents graves saying, "Mom, Dad Rest In Peace." She was 17 year old and now responsible for her 14-year-old brother and her 10-year-old sister.

Rosa and her brother Rudolf worked in the forest and their sister Bertha stayed in the barracks waiting for their return. After a meeting between Krushev and the German Counselor, Dr. Adenauer, the Commandatur (harsh rules and regulations) was removed; Rosa and her siblings were able to move to Asia to get away from the terrible cold in Siberia. After years of applying, permission to move to Germany finally was granted.

I also had the opportunity to visit with my other cousin, Amalie Marchel (nee Roth). With some of her family Amalie was able to return to Germany. She was telling of the cruel life in the camps as Poland was overrun with the Russian Army. The German people were treated very cruel. The German people were stripped of everything they still had. The Polish and Russians would come into the camps at night. People were sleeping on straw laid floor in barracks. The Russian and Polish Army personnel would shine a flashlight in the prisoners' faces, take the young girls away, rape and molest them. Amalie was telling me with tears in her eyes, "Anna, I'm not ashamed to tell you that I was raped, not once, but several times while in the camps in Poland." One could hear the young girls crying out for their mothers during the night. Their mothers were powerless against the soldiers. Amalie told me that her own mother was trying to intervene. Her mother begged for the soldiers to take her instead, she wanted her daughter Amalie to be spared. Her mother ended up with a hard beating, and Amalie had to do what was asked of her to stay alive. As the Russian and Polish were taking Amalie away, struggling to get free, she was taken to a barn and beaten and raped over and over. She lay unconscious from her beating, and was found stripped naked from the waist down by women in the early morning who were going to milk the cows. One woman saw a pile of straw and something beneath. She took a pitchfork and poked into the straw and poked her body. Amalie started crying, semi-consciously. She didn't know where she was. Her face was black and blue, swollen from the beatings. The women took Amalie back to the camp, where they helped wash her face. There were no doctors to give medical attention. It took several days for Amalie to be able to open her eyes. She looked into a mirror, and she broke down in tears, crying her heart out asking, "What have we done to deserve this treatment?" The molestations of young girls went on night after night. One day they were taken to a train station and loaded in freight train boxcars. The boxcar was packed with people, like sardines. The boxcars were cold as winter was nearing. They parted from Poland and went for long stretches at a time without stopping. A big pail was supplied to use as an outhouse. The stench was unbearable. They went days without a piece of bread to be divided amongst the boxcar load of people. By pushing deeper into the unknown, upon arrival in Siberia in1945, all young and old were forced to work in the forest. Loudspeakers were sounded for everyone to get up and go to work. They were treated worse then animals, with nothing to eat, and so miserably cold. Her mother, sister Katja and brother Daniel died of starvation in Siberia. Amalia's story was heart breaking and very emotional.

Our trip was now nearing to an end and was time to fly back to Canada. I will always cherish the time I had to be able to talk to my relatives once more.

Everyone has his or her own story to tell. We all had different experiences, but yet similar as to the brutal way a human race was treated. I still live in Medicine Hat, Alberta and continue to enjoy the freedom Canada has to offer.

Afterward

Since I started writing this book I located two more cousins that escaped Siberia. I had no contact with them, not knowing where they were for 65 years. They ended up in Northern Germany and I am currently in touch with both of them.